SPIRITUAL INTIMACY AND COMMUNITY

SPIRITUAL INTIMACY AND COMMUNITY

An Ignatian View of the Small Faith Community

John English SJ

Darton, Longman and Todd
London

First published in 1992 by
Darton, Longman and Todd Ltd
89 Lillie Road, London SW6 1UD

ISBN 0–232–51992–7

A catalogue record for this book is available
from the British Library

Cover: Judy Linard

Phototypeset by Intype, London
Printed and bound in Great Britain
at the University Press, Cambridge

To Bernadette
and those small faith groups of Jesuits and CLCs
with whom I have shared many intimate
spiritual conversations

CONTENTS

PREFACE

For many years I have been involved in helping individuals understand and develop their interior life in terms of their relationship
with God. I have assisted them in learning and practising various
approaches to prayer: scriptural reading, meditation, contemplation, and methods of finding God in all things. The basic instrument that I have used for this is the *Spiritual Exercises* of St Ignatius
Loyola.[1] The spirituality I have promoted is Ignatian spirituality.
It is an active this-world spirituality. Ignatian spirituality acknowledges God's active presence in developing more truthful, loving,
just and peaceful structures for the betterment of humanity. Those
who give themselves to this spirituality are filled with desire to take
on the mind and heart of Christ and be instruments of God's grace
in this world.

As I accompanied individuals on their spiritual journey I became
aware that many of them were approaching a dead end. For some
this happened because they were only concerned about their one-
on-one relationship with Christ. Some thought they could save the
world by their individualistic efforts. Some were unable to realize
their desires because they were caught in dysfunctional structures.
As I reflected and prayed about this phenomenon I came to the
conviction that one can fully understand Ignatian spirituality only
by taking account of the communal dimension. People needed to
understand and experience Ignatius' principles and methods of
prayer in a communal setting. In fact, they were first developed
and applied in such a setting. When the earliest companions – the
men who would eventually found the Jesuit order – began to form
a community in the 1530s during their years of study at the University of Paris, they made serious deliberations not by merely seeking
a majority opinion, but by coming to a unanimous position. Javier
Osuna SJ writes:[2]

They find there the essential element, which is the will of God communicated to the group as a result of community discernment. They have then complete trust that the Spirit will speak to the group discerning in common. In this dialogue the minority takes on an important position of its own, since the voice of the Spirit must be discerned in them too . . . For a group that has no superior the decision-making process is communal discernment: the decisions are taken by all . . . They seek the will of God in the group itself as it deliberates in prayer.

I have come to believe that we take on the fullness of the mind and heart of Christ and become instruments of God's grace in our world when we acknowledge the communal dimension and seek to live Christian community rather than imaging ourselves as isolated units. Ignatian spirituality emphasizes loving action, and I believe that we are seeing a renewal of the consciousness that we do not create grace-filled structures by working alone. God calls us to community.

This led me to experiment with ways in which groups of people might use the Ignatian dynamic to help them discern their decisions and actions. The staff of Loyola House in Guelph, Ontario, began to develop communal spiritual exercises, working with parish staffs, bishops' diocesan senates, and councils of religious men and women. Eventually a co-operative venture was set up with other spiritual centres in North America to investigate and develop Ignatian communal exercises.[3]

Over the last fifteen years I have discovered that many people have come to realize that the gospel message is basically for the totality of humanity and that only a communal approach to spirituality and the Christian life is a valid expression of this reality. This has led me to the conviction that all Christians are deeply moved by a desire for community, yet often we seem to be incapable of achieving it to any great degree.

From experience in my family and parishes where I have lived and served as a priest and from life in the Society of Jesus and some of its small communities as well as in Christian Life Communities, I know that Christian community in its deepest sense can be realized. I think that many Christians do not believe this. I also suspect that many Christians do not know what is meant by Christian community let alone how to achieve it. Many do not even recognize the possibility of sharing life with a small faith community – in spite of their hunger for it. In this book I present an instrument to assist Christians in creating and developing Christian community. I hope that this book will facilitate this possibility. Maybe, too, some readers will experience a conversion of mind and heart and be able to recognize God's presence in all humanity and in a small Christian faith community.

There are various levels of conversion that express the intimate presence of God in each person: the sense of being creature; the sense of forgiven sinner; the sense of call to discipleship; the practice of discernment of spirits; union with Christ in suffering and joy. Some of these are healing experiences and some are discipleship experiences.

There is also a level of conversion that has to do with the spiritual significance of the faith community for us. There is first a recognition coming from an intellectual conversion regarding the gospel message. Second, there is the heightened awareness of the presence of God in all humanity and in this specific faith community. Third, there is the willingness to respond to this awareness. And fourth, the conversion to community is experienced as growth in the practice of spiritual discernment by the community.

As the reader will recognize, I am greatly indebted to many communities and individuals. Among these are my companions in the Society of Jesus, the Loyola House team of 1973–86, the group known as ISECP (Ignatian Spiritual Exercises for the Corporate Person), and the many Christian Life Communities in Canada who have shared their lives with me. I would like to thank a number of people for assisting me to get this book into print. First among these is Bruce Henry SJ, who spent many hours helping me to organize this material and being the overall editor of the book. The following persons have read the manuscript and given me useful comments: Sr Lavinia Byrne IBVM, Jack Costello SJ, David Fleming SJ, George Schemel SJ and Phil Shano SJ. My thanks are also due to Jennifer Wild, and to Morag Reeve at Darton, Longman and Todd.

[1] The translation I have used is that of Elisabeth Meier Tetlow: *The Spiritual Exercises of St Ignatius Loyola, A New Translation* (University Press of America, Lanham, MA, 1987). References to the numbered sections of the *Spiritual Exercises* are given in the form: Exx 1.

[2] Javier Osuna sj: 'Friends in the Lord', *The Way*, Series 3 (1974), p. 57. Osuna gives a detailed description of this small lay faith community making decisions about its life and ministry.

[3] Through a co-operative venture mainly between the spiritual centres of Guelph, ON and Wernersville, PA the program and manual *Ignatian Spiritual Exercises for the Corporate Person* came into being. These communal exercises have now been presented in many countries throughout the world. Cf. George Schemel sj (ed.): *Ignatian Spiritual Exercises for the Corporate Person* (University of Scranton, Scranton, PA 18510, ISECP Group, 1990).

John Wickham sj, coming out of the same conviction, has also developed a different series of communal spiritual exercises in two volumes. Cf. John Wickham sj: *The Common Faith* and *The Communal Exercises* (Ignatian Centre of Spirituality, Montreal, 1988).

INTRODUCTION

We are only persons at all through our relations with other persons.
(John Macmurray)

It seems to have been necessary for the church in Europe and North America to return to the individual interior life for a sense of Christian identity and as a basis for outgoing gospel action. This was certainly true in the period following Vatican II. I am, however, concerned that we, the spiritual guides and leaders, have neglected the believing community, which provides the more basic experience of identity and gospel action.

We know that the teachings of the Hebrew and the Christian scriptures emphasize that our faith is a communal affair. It is the believing *community* that in Hebrew and Christian Testaments alike is the object of God's saving love, and the subject of the covenant relationship with God. This can be seen not only in the great promises of Exodus 6:6 ('I am the LORD . . . I shall free you . . . I shall redeem you . . . I shall take you as my people and I shall be your God'), but (for example) also in the thought of Hosea, who envisages God as addressing the people of Israel as God's wife and God's child (Hos 2:14; 11:1,3,4). Jeremiah too, in spite of his heightened self-awareness and his sense of isolation, still sees God's continuous love for *Israel*: 'Within them I shall plant my law, writing it on their hearts. Then I shall be their God and they will be my people' (Jr 31:33).[1]

The vine symbolism in John 15 suggests the covenant-community of Jesus with his disciples; and Paul's image of the Christian community as the body of Christ also emphasizes the communal (1 Co 12:12,13,27).

In spite of this, the following statements seem to be true of many Christians:

1

- The understanding and practice of spirituality have tended to focus on the individual person's experience and aspirations.
- Communal attitudes are not considered as vital to the ultimate meaning of our lives.
- We do not appreciate the communal as significant for personal salvation or for discovering the will of God in our interior life and in the building of the divine–human community here and now.
- When we think about personal salvation and leading a fully Christian life we are still governed by individualistic images and desires.
- Our image of God is as someone 'out there', a god we need to please, or a god who performs miracles or a god who loves and condemns us as single entities.
- We still operate from an 'I' position with God.
- We are fascinated by a psychological understanding of ourselves as independent units in our world.
- We do not appreciate the historical and communal in spiritual matters.
- We have very little interest in the church as community.
- We are not sure what a Christian faith community is.
- We do not do much communal discernment.
- We lack conviction about the significance of communal discernment, often actually seeing it as an attack on personal freedom, personal discernment and personal decision-making.
- We think communal discernment is only a matter of a group process that eventually leads to consensus.
- We do not easily relate and refer to other groups, e.g., peace groups, justice groups, governmental agencies and the United Nations, to help us search or to be objective discerners in our own personal and communal actions.

In contrast, I believe that it needs to be affirmed that:

- Community is a lived reality and not just a mental construct.
- Community is more than a collectivity of human beings. It is a corporate person. For a Christian the term 'body of Christ' expresses at once an organic and a personal sense of unity. There is a connection with the ancient Hebrew idea of

2

'corporate personality' and at the same time a new beginning in Christ (cf. Paul's Adam–Jesus analogy).

- Community and communal experience are as primary as personal effort and experience in living out our Christian life and discerning the will of God in our personal lives.

- The person is constituted and known by relationship and has a social or communal component. Only in community does the individual find and appreciate personhood.[2]

- If spirituality focuses on the experiences the individual has in, through and of community, there is less danger of an individualistic spirituality.

- All the great spiritual desires, hopes, truths, maxims, experiences of 'consolation' and 'desolation', that have been identified through the centuries can be applied to a community of persons.[3]

- Communal spiritual discernment is an instrument for developing true Christian community. It gives an experiential understanding of the spiritual life that is more complete than that yielded by the present-day emphasis on the individual.

- Communal discernment is a necessity; its basic experience is spiritual consolation, and to draw out the meaning and implications of this expression and this claim is a primary task of the present book.

Flow of the book

In chapter 1, 'The Desire for Christian Community', I consider the significance of the multitude of small Christian faith communities appearing in the church today. I discuss the changes in the images of self, God and humanity that the new spirituality engenders and the ways communal discernment enhances this new sense of identity.

The next chapter, 'What is Spiritual Discernment?', continues the topic of the place of communal discernment in the establishing, developing and growth of small inclusive, intimate Christian faith communities. Through a discussion of an example of communal discernment the chapter demonstrates how reflection on experiences of communal spiritual consolation in a group heightens awareness of its new sense of identity and being in relationship with God, self, members and humanity, and how this awareness becomes both an instrument for developing this identity and for doing communal discernment.

The next chapter, 'The Secret of Communal Discernment: Recognizing Spiritual Consolation', discusses the main purposes of spiritual discernment and then moves to the process of discernment in general. It shows how continual use of communal discernment as a way of life creates community.

Chapter 4, 'Establishing Christian Community: The Story Component', considers the activity of sharing our personal and communal graced history. It elaborates the significance of this activity as a community continues to grow and discusses the requisite skills as well as the practice and experience of sharing story in relation to communal discernment.

Chapter 5, 'The Challenge of Expressing our Story', stresses the significance of public disclosure for the growth and development of community, and suggests both what to express from a faith perspective and how to express it.

'Communal Spiritual Freedom', chapter 6, focuses on our freedom as beloved sinners. It deals with our limitations and sinfulness when making decisions regarding future actions. It suggests ways we can grow freely into a new sense of identity as a beloved community of God.

The next chapter, 'Intimate Knowledge of Jesus from Contemplating Christ among Us', considers one of the activities of Christian discernment that will assist a group to grow more fully into a Christian community, that of growing into intimate knowledge of the mind and heart of Jesus Christ as community members develop deeper relationships with each other.

Chapter 8, 'The Discernment Process of a Community of Disciples', faces the challenge that authentic Christian community must be a community of service with Christ for the betterment of humanity. It considers the activity of discerning decisions for actions whose concern is beyond the group itself and the ways in which such discernment helps a community to develop.

Chapter 9, 'Confirmation', focuses on the communal process of discerning experiences of confirmation of decisions. It considers the significance of seeking confirmation for the growth of a group. I describe confirmation, the occasions for confirmation, and ways a group might seek confirmation. Then I discuss the place of consensus in communal decision making.

Chapter 10, 'The Continual Way of Communal Spiritual Discernment', develops the awareness that spiritual discernment is not a once-in-a-lifetime experience but a way of life. Many of the insights and instruments of previous chapters are gathered together to assist a group in adopting ongoing communal discernment.

'Celebrating a Continuous Way of Life of Communal Intimacy with God', chapter 11, discusses the importance of celebration as part of a community's discerning activity. As it continues its decision-making process the community is encouraged to recognize that it is gifted by God and a gift for others. Celebrating this giftedness may be understood as a special form of prayer often referred to as 'application of the senses' (Exx 121–6).

Throughout this book there are some basic assumptions. Building on the foundations of the ordinary Christian belief system as articulated in the creed, I believe that:

- Life is most fully understood from a Christian faith perspective.
- This faith perspective can assist us in understanding our human experience.
- The Holy Spirit is operative in our human experiences.
- To appreciate our relationship with God we need a heightened sensitivity to the ways God relates to us in an intimate (personally affective) manner.
- Through such sensitivity we can begin to discern the various motions that take place in our inner being.
- Such discernment includes both private and public, individual and communal experiences.
- Recognizing and deciding from the interrelationship of these levels of discernment is important for our world today.
- The process and experience of communally discerned decisions and actions is an effective instrument for establishing, developing and continuing a committed Christian faith community.

- Committed Christian faith communities are necessarily inclusive and dedicated to the betterment of humanity.

NOTES

[1] Except where indicated, scripture references are taken from the *New Jerusalem Bible* (Darton, Longman and Todd, London, 1985), with occasional slight alterations to make the language inclusive.

[2] Cf. many writings of the philosopher John Macmurray on the realization and experience of persons. The sentence at the head of this introduction is from *Freedom in the Modern World* (Faber, London, 1932); cf. also 'We overcome individualism by communal action . . . It is only in meeting others that we find ourselves and our own reality' (*Search for Reality in Religion*, Quaker, London, 1965).

[3] For the last eight years I have been discussing and experiencing the validity of this statement with James Borbely sj, Marita Carew RSHM, John Haley, Judith Roemer and George Schemel sj. To assist spiritual guides of groups we have composed the manual referred to on page xii, *Ignatian Spiritual Exercises for the Corporate Person* (University of Scranton, Scranton, PA 18510, 1990). Further references to this work will use the acronym *ISECP*.

THE DESIRE FOR CHRISTIAN COMMUNITY

It is the understanding [of a 'soft individualism'] expressed by those in the fellowship of Alcoholics Anonymous . . . that permits ourselves to seep out and the selves of others to seep in.

(M. Scott Peck)[1]

It is an extraordinary phenomenon indeed, the welling up of small faith communities throughout the Christian world!

The phenomenon is manifest in the many different ways in which Christians are attempting to form small faith communities, some in well organized common living together, others in less organized living together, still others not living together. There are married people and singles living in rural and city communes. There are communities of marginalized persons such as L'Arche communities. There are persons attempting to live community outside such settings, connected with each other in groups such as Cursillo, Charismatic Renewal, Marriage Encounter, Christian Life Community (CLC), Christian Family Movement (CFM), and twelve-step groups such as Alcoholics Anonymous and Adult Children of Alcoholics. There are small groups of persons living in large institutions of vowed religious life. Other groups of vowed religious are moving away from institutional settings into smaller houses.

I have seen groups get formed in various ways. For example, a person at a charismatic meeting says, 'I am feeling the need of intimate community.' Others respond to this outburst. People come together then not so much to share intimately their interior life, but to commit themselves more intimately to each other.

Often the desire for community goes through stages. For example, six people who are heavily committed to the social and psychological care of people in prisons felt a need to share some of the burdens of this work from a faith perspective. As they shared their need for advice and support they became conscious that deeper desires were operating in their beings, and they realized that they really wanted to support each other in prayer. This they did for some time. Gradually they expressed two other important desires: the desire for a fuller commitment to each other in a communal way and the desire to assist each other in personal decisions. Eventually they realized that this last desire meant a further entrance into each other's faith life so that they could truly assist each other in making significant decisions. As the group continued to gather it met other faith concerns such as the desire to be instruments of God's grace in working to create more just structures in the prison system.

Reading the phenomenon

To understand the phenomenon, for several years I have surveyed participants in small faith communities. Here are some responses to my questions.

What are you seeking in small communities? What has led you to seek a small faith community?

- 'I've been through many programmes of prayer and am looking for a more permanent way of Christian life.'
- 'My life has been so hectic in social action groups, I'm looking for a deeper relationship with Christ.'
- 'I find that I am all alone in my faith.'
- 'I'm here because a friend invited me.'
- 'I wanted a group with whom to share and be energized for deeper involvement in Christian social action.'

What do you do in these small communities?

- 'We listen to scripture and share our understanding of it.'
- 'We recount the experiences of our life since we last met, using a Christian viewpoint as we talk and listen.'
- 'We talk over some of our problems in life and try to help each other with them in terms of our Christian faith.'

- 'We help each other with personal decisions on the basis of our faith.'
- 'We socialize every so often.'
- 'We make some group decisions on social action issues or assisting people who need our help.'
- 'We discuss ways of living our Christian faith in our professions or places of work.'

What are you personally experiencing?

- 'I experience a sense of belonging.'
- 'I sense that I am welcome here even though I am a sinner.'
- 'I am getting a new knowledge of Jesus, myself and others.'
- 'I am beginning to have a new awareness of Christ in our midst and to appreciate Jesus' words: "Where two or three are gathered in my name, there am I in the midst of them." '
- 'At times I feel really challenged by the group, but for the most part in a supportive way.'

How would you describe your community?

- 'It's a small Christian group sharing experiences of life out of prayer and faith.'
- 'It is a group with whom I can discuss some of the deep faith issues that the world today makes me face.'
- 'It is a small group of religious attempting to support each other through sharing and prayer to live out their commitment.'
- 'It is a place to get help to live my faith.'
- 'I feel very free and able to share quite intimately some of my deep religious beliefs and some of my fears and sinfulness.'
- 'I find our group a concerned group of persons wishing to bring into our discussion and consideration all of the many issues that face humanity today.'

The meaning of the phenomenon: the motives

The reasons people establish or seek out small faith communities are as complex as the persons coming together. Among the deeper desires that attract people to form a small faith community is the need of a forum for reflecting on questions and situations relating to home life, work and apostolic activity. The emphasis in some groups is on shared reflection and mutual support; others are drawn together by a desire for united action. Participation in a small community gives people a sense of belonging, regardless of sinfulness, and fulfils a desire to grow in knowledge of Christ and self. Some small communities are founded in reaction to the competitiveness, powerlessness and individualistic life–style of industrial culture in Europe and North America and to its secular atheism; or to injustice in Latin America, Africa and Asia. But these same circumstances can also lead people to seek community as a positive response to the larger peace and justice issues that the total society has to face – human rights, poverty, the polluted environment, contaminated food, starvation or multinational media control.

These communities are a source of new life, energy, unity and hope as well as a re-expression of the life we imagine the first Christians to have experienced in the early church. They indicate a deep desire for something not found in the large institutional churches and in the rest of the culture. Christians seek deeper experiences of intimacy that only the sharing of personal faith life can give. There is, too, a new conviction among us that the faith is to be an instrument to bring about a more just and peaceful society in this world rather than solely a preparation for life after death; and a belief that community is the way to live out Christian commitment in today's world.

People are looking for something that their family, social life and work situation do not provide. Apparently the parish itself as well as other Christian organizations that encourage participation in a devotional life or activity of a charitable or social form are not enough. Some speak of having a vocation to community. Others are convinced that their own experience is important and they want a faith context in which to share their experience. They have a deep desire to live the Christian life in the midst of their family and work context and not to escape from the world, bombarded as it is by materialism. They have experienced a disenchantment with individualistic and privatized Christianity. They come together for a communal and public expression of their faith. Some people wish to bring true Christian values and practice into oppressive structures wherever they encounter them. Eventually these needs, desires and commitments are the dynamic by which each small community creates its own traditions, structures and ways of growth.

Despite great variety in motives, life situations and character of groups, two dimensions occur in everyone's experience of small Christian faith community: *intimacy* and *inclusivity*.

Intimacy is not just a matter of the size of the group, although smallness seems to be a necessary condition for Christian intimacy. People seek intimacy in a faith context to counteract the isolation, ostracism and insignificance they experience as they try to live more fully the Christian life. While there is some comfort in belonging to a large church structure, the present state of our world is demanding a context for intimate sharing and witnessing of the Christian faith. So people seek a forum and mode for expressing intimately the meaning of their Christian faith and concerns that arise in their lives. People desire a context of trust where they can risk vulnerability and self-revelation, a context that permits critical evaluation of personal and communal life. People want a context in which they can fulfil their desire to live a real faith before humanity and where their critical reflection will find positive support.

The second basic characteristic of today's small Christian communities is inclusivity, but not in the sense that they will grow to become parishes or encourage large gatherings. Rather, they open out to the world in a way which is not élitist or exclusive. Although small, these groups tend to be inclusive of all people and concerned for the betterment of the human race. Today's small Christian faith communities tend to have a service or mission orientation, coming out of a sense of equality and fellowship with all other humans.

The church's position

While each small community has its own reasons for existing, churches see the desire for Christian community as an activity of the Holy Spirit working in human hearts. And although these expressions of community are new, the desire for Christian community is as old as Christ. Desires are to be tested to see if they come from God (1 Jn 4:1). The affirmation and encouraging of the development of small communities by the church confirms that these desires are an expression of the Holy Spirit.

The desire for and development of small communities is in tune with the experience of the early church. In the first indication of community between Jesus and the apostles as portrayed by St John (cf. Jn 1:35–9), questions are asked: ' "What do you want?" . . . "Rabbi, . . . where do you live?" ' The questions are followed by an answer and a description: ' "Come and see"; . . . so they went and stayed with him that day.' The oldness and newness are present in the elements of inclusiveness, intimacy, smallness and sharing of faith.

Within the Roman Catholic communion the phenomenon of small faith communities has been recognized even at Bishops' Synods. After the Vatican Synod on the Laity in 1987 those who attended referred to the whole church and each parish as a community of communities. The synod recognized and encouraged this movement:

> The freedom for lay people in the Church to form groups is to be acknowledged. Such liberty is a true and proper right that . . . flows from the sacrament of baptism, which calls the lay faithful to participate actively in the Church's communion and mission.
>
> (*Christifideles Laici* #29)

Vatican II in its process of returning to the early church's experience acknowledged the significance of community. It did this especially in its descriptions of the church and the Eucharist.

> Truly partaking of the body of the Lord in the breaking of the eucharistic bread, we are taken up into communion with him and with one another. 'Because the bread is one, we though many are one body, all of us who partake of the one bread' (1 Co 10:17).

12

In this way all of us are made members of his body (cf. 1 Co 12:27), 'but severally members one of another' (Rm 12:5).

(*Lumen Gentium* #7)

Images of community

Down the centuries we see, in however generalized a way, a sequence in the development of Christian community life which is reflected in the development of present-day small communities of faith. A selective survey of the history of Christian communities tends to display an initial exclusiveness (cf. e.g. the Pauline communities), becoming more self-confident and combative in times of persecution. In later centuries, as the church became accepted into the larger political structure, self-contained community was sought away from public life (in monasticism), or as a support to or refuge between forays into the market-place (in the time of the rise of the mendicant orders). The contribution of Ignatius Loyola in the sixteenth century was to promote faith communities that image themselves as gatherings to discern the presence of Christ everywhere. The emphasis is on recognizing what is happening, so as to follow the lead of the Spirit in the context of the whole life of humankind.

Communities of this sort are apostolic men and women intent on being instruments of God's goodness in the world. It is a model that is being revived in our day, in the aftermath of Pope John XXIII's opening of the windows of the church. In the ensuing storm we may be able to sustain the fight for good in the midst of the fray by belonging to discerning communities.

An ideal small faith community in today's world may be close to Ignatius' concept and image; but each community will have to begin, develop and grow in ways similar to that of the larger faith community. So we will see at the beginning some initial form of conversion to the significance of community. After this the group will tend to become exclusive and to see itself basically as a support group. In time the members will see themselves as persons who go out to evangelize and then return to their support group for insight and strength. Eventually, the image of the community becomes that of a discerning apostolic group. They see themselves as a united community which discerns its activity within the larger experience of humanity. It reflects on its interior faith experiences while reading the signs of the times. It now images itself as being a discerning community within the world where God is present and as encouraging humanity to develop a more loving, peaceful and just world community.

A new spirituality

The phenomenon of small Christian communities welling up everywhere indicates an intuition of the possibility of a new Christian spirituality in today's world.

Christians are responding to the urging of the Holy Spirit calling us to live a spirituality of intimate community. This means that Christians realize anew that life is a community affair, that salvation is a community experience, and that building the realm of God here on earth is a community endeavour. They judge the affairs of life in terms of community relationships. They understand scriptural messages of creation, sin, forgiveness, call, suffering and glory in terms of community. The desires and petitions of prayer are of the community. Prayer is a community experience. People experience, understand and judge life in the relationships between individuals and the community and realize life in the individual members and in the community as a whole.

Today's communal spirituality is in the tradition of the early church and expresses a deep appreciation of the church as the body of Christ. Although there are different styles of Christian living in these various gatherings of Christians, a common spirituality is present in all of them. What images and self-identities are present? What way of life is operative? In other words, what is the spirituality of Christian community?

Person: images and identity

If I live a spirituality of community a change takes place in the way I image myself. I grasp my identity and person in a different way. I place high regard on interdependency, on the relationships I have with others. If one believes that one's identity is the result of interpersonal relationships, then one images oneself basically as a being in relationship. Religious experiences which bring about a conversion in one's sense of identity and change one's preferred way of living are appreciated as communal. The person recognizes these experiences in terms of relationship with other persons. Sometimes, too, the religious experiences themselves are communal.

Community is an expression of persons. I know myself in and through my relationships with others. As we consider communal spirituality, we must be careful not to dichotomize or set up a duality between each person and community.[2]

All true spirituality enhances, recognizes, moves from and moves toward the human person.[3] I am a person first, a creature. Knowledge of my identity comes through reflection on my experience of other persons and all creation. The self-image that one has *vis-à-vis* God, other humans and the whole of creation is foundational to one's spirituality.

Religious experiences are especially important because they bring about a conversion in one's perspective on life. The result is a change in how one images self, Christian community, humanity, creation and God. Considered from the vantage point of spirituality, the images that we have of ourselves are more than mere words. They express a totality of ourselves. They are a symbol of ourselves in the same sense that the creed is a symbol of the whole Catholic faith. Identity has an interior quality. For Christians the realization and heightened awareness of the indwelling Spirit is an expression of identity.

Identity of Christian community

Belonging to a Christian community gives the members a new sense of personal identity, and Christian community is dependent on the members having a communal identity. This sense of identity is in the members and in the group as a whole.

The community realizes its identity as an experience of the presence of the risen Christ in its midst, whether reflected upon and expressed or not. This identity calls forth a sense of unity and responsibility to the Holy Spirit's activity within and beyond it to the benefit of all humanity.

This suggests that any group of Christians that comes together with the intention of doing something for the good of humanity is a Christian community. Yet there is a difference between a Christian group and a Christian community, which is found in the sense of self-identity shared by the members, that is, their interior sense of unity and responsibility. The sense of unity is the special unity of covenant. The sense of responsibility is communal and involves communal spiritual discernment in the decision-making of the whole group.

The change that happens when a group becomes a Christian community is in the locale of Christ. Members begin to experience Christ differently. He is no longer 'up there in heaven' or 'out there' in the blessed sacrament. This usually means more of a horizontal, historical, or present awareness of Christ in our midst and as mystical body, without denying his otherness.

The community accepts that the Trinity is active in our lives, constantly creating, healing, freeing, encouraging, calling us forth, uniting with us in sorrows and joys, in trials and triumphs, in good and bad times. But we look for this action in a communal way rather than in an individualistic way. St Augustine's comment on 1 Jn 4:16 is to the point:

> God is love, and he who dwells in love is dwelling in God. Love your neighbour therefore, and observe the source of that love in you; there, as best you can, you will see God.[4]

As persons grow in their experience of communal spirituality, they come to a new way of relating to liturgical prayer and the scriptures. Members of community can resonate with the prayer over the gifts at the Eucharist: 'Lord, hear the prayers of your people and receive our gifts. May the worship of each one here bring salvation to all.'[5] Many of the scripture texts about Christ identifying with people take on new meaning. For example, the light–darkness theme and the in-and-out-of-Christ theme in John's first letter now have to do precisely with our relationships with other persons and are not just vertical viewpoints (cf. 1 Jn 2:8–11).

Only with time do members of a group come to a communal awareness of who they are. This occurs as individuals begin to reach out to others in the group and start finding new personal identity through identifying with the others. As community identity starts to come into being a new level of intimacy is experienced. Members now begin to risk their reputations with the others in the group. They admit to limitations, fears, sinfulness. Now they share all the aspects of their personal history, they help each other understand their stories of the way God has been at work in their lives – the failures as well as the successes, the sufferings as well as the joys, the sinfulness as well as the blessedness, the shadow as well as the light, the 'destructive moods' as well as the 'creative moods'.[6] The members become more willing to commit themselves to communal prayer, discussion, decision and action. Gradually the group's concerns become the individual's concern. Prayer moves from individual to communal concerns. The community grows in acceptance of its corporate humanity. Deeper interchange in the community heightens each member's acceptance of the human. Individuals recognize in a new way the human Jesus of the scriptures and the significance of Jesus' life as a paradigm for their own lives. Eventually they move to a recognition and acceptance that Christ is present and found in this faith community of Christians in spite of its faults and weaknesses.

They find their identity in terms of membership in this faith community. Their lives are understood and grasped as experiences shared with other persons. In time they will image themselves as freely committed members of the body of the risen Christ who is present and operative in this world.

When the group senses that the giftedness of the community is more than the sum of individual gifts it may sense its existence as coming from beyond itself and be amazed that it has gathered together in the Lord's name. As the group senses that its sinfulness is greater than the sum of individual sins it may be led to a sense of sorrow for communal sinfulness. This sense of identity may lead the group to seek forgiveness for its own sinful social structures or its complicity with sinful social structures beyond itself.

17

From such awareness the group enters more deeply into the mystery of Christian community. People are given new understandings and new perspectives on the Christian life, new horizons. They gradually develop their common vision; life is grasped as a communal enterprise rather than an individual one. All the members realize that they are not left alone to cope with the mystery of life, but that they belong to a community of faith-filled persons interested in each other's welfare. Their life is experienced as fellowship. This is supportive and energizing: common acceptance gives a sense of support; common ideals, values and goals give hope-filled energy. People discover that the Christian life is a communal endeavour and that their life in Christ is to be found in the ways they interact with other persons in the faith community and beyond it with the whole human race. St Paul's prayer is to the point: 'May the Lord increase and enrich your love for each other and for all, so that it matches ours for you' (1 Th 3:12). A new sensitivity to the presence of God and Christ in communal life grows, along with a new interpretation and appreciation of the person and message of Jesus Christ and the rest of the Christian Testament. People find the risen Christ in their midst. They realize that the risen Christ can live in the weaknesses, sufferings and energy experienced in community. Such a group is now free to appreciate Christian community and to respond to the Spirit's call for themselves and all humanity.

Community and covenant

Christian community is also an experience of *koinonia*, Christian fellowship. The sense of community contained in companionship in the Lord is well described in scripture. From a Christian point of view the description of the early church in the Acts of the Apostles gives us the clearest expression of this companionship. The sharing of everything (property, food, prayer, miraculous powers and the good news of Jesus Christ) was the sign of their communion with each other in the Lord. Such Christian fellowship involves a covenant relationship of Christ with the church and the human race.

A major distinction between a group and a community is that a

18

group does not have the same type of commitment to itself that a community has. Commitments are expressed by *contracts* or *covenants*. Whether contract arrangements can express community is a moot point. Contracts involve a give-and-take arrangement. The parties pay in one form or another for goods or services rendered. In a covenant arrangement the parties share their goods, talents and lives. Ideally, covenant is the sharing of each other's person.

Covenant is a dominant theme in the Hebrew Testament. God said to Noah, 'When I gather the clouds over the earth and the bow appears in the clouds, I shall recall the covenant between myself and you and every living creature, in a word all living things' (Gn 9:14, 15), and to Abraham, 'I shall make you a great nation, I shall bless you' (Gn 12:2). To Moses God said, 'I am now making a covenant: I shall work . . . wonders at the head of your whole people . . .' (Ex 34:10), and to the psalmist, 'I have made a covenant with my Chosen One, sworn an oath to my servant David' (Ps 89:3).

It is on the basis of his appreciation of God's covenant with Abraham, Isaac, Jacob, Moses and David that Jesus gives himself to God and to the human race. Recognizing an identity between his person and his life-blood, Jesus proclaims his personal faithfulness and presence to the believing community which celebrates his death and resurrection. At the Last Supper he gives the memorial rite of his covenant (Lk 22:19–20).

In its Eucharist the church celebrates this covenant between itself and Christ and urges this kind of bonding between its members. Today covenant is known by the bonding that exists among persons in a community. I am aware of one community in which the members see each other as caring for each other's children, sharing goods and visiting each other when they are sick, much as a loving parent, brother or sister might do. In this community the persons commit themselves to carry each other's burdens, their joys and fears, their successes and failures, their sufferings and disappointments. We recognize the difference in level of commitment in a group such as this, from that of many voluntary groups of people who come together for sociability or ministerial action.

Covenant is important for orders of religious men and women. The members of such communities dedicate their persons and lives to the order. Within this covenant there are contract arrangements.

The methods of coming to decision and the parameters of the vows indicate some of these.

In the small faith communities welling up in the church there are likewise aspects of contract and covenant. Contract usually surfaces in terms of time commitment to meetings and dues. Covenant is present with the sharing of goods and actions. Covenant is most present at the time of deeper sharing of one's inner life with others. At this time members are conscious that they can risk themselves and know they are fully accepted. Covenant is also at play when members support other members of the group who may be suffering. The sense of covenant disappears when confidentiality is broken or members feel they can no longer belong to the group because it is moving too fast or not moving fast enough.

Initially the idea of covenant is quite frightening to us. Intimate relationship among members of a community takes time. We need to call upon our faith: covenant is achieved by the action of the Holy Spirit freeing people, giving them a sense of trust with each other. It is not for nothing that St Paul speaks about the bonding of married partners in terms of covenant. 'Love one another', says Jesus in John 15:12, 'as I have loved you.'

Exercises

There are a number of spiritual exercises that a group can do to assist it in its communal life. At the end of each chapter some exercises are given to help a community assimilate the matter of each chapter. The steps in the exercises have various purposes. First, there are hymns and scripture to help a group settle into the presence of God. Second, there is calling to mind what we want from God (the grace we desire). Third, there is expressing to each other and listening to each other express what we have discovered in our prayer or our life experiences. Fourth, there is acknowledgement of the contribution of others to one's own life and action.

EXERCISE I: DISCLOSING ONE'S INNER BEING TO OTHERS

Some knowledge of the interior life of all the members of a group is necessary if it wishes to be a discerning community. An exercise in which persons reflect on certain intimate religious experiences in their lives and then share them is a good instrument to help the members of a group disclose their interior lives to the others.

This exercise has three parts: some periods of personal prayer with one's religious experiences, preparing oneself to share the results of prayer, and sharing the results of this prayer when the group meets.

Theme: I am the beloved of God

PERSONAL PRAYER

Context

You are my son, the Beloved; my favour rests on you. (Mk 1:11)

I have loved you just as the Father has loved me. Remain in my love. (cf. Jn 15:8–10)

There is no need to be afraid, little flock, for it has pleased your Father to give you the kingdom. (cf. Lk 12:22–32)

I imagine myself hearing the Lord speak these words to me.

The grace desired

I want and desire a deep awareness that I am God's beloved, so that I may have a deep trust and confidence in the Lord's constant love and concern for me.

Points

For Jesus the experience at his baptism gave him an awareness of who he was in relation to God, the Father. It contained his sense

21

of identity and vocation, the base from which he could live out the rest of his life.

I make myself present with Jesus at his baptism. (Lk 3:21–2)

I review my life and recall experiences that indicate to me that I am the beloved of God.

Aware of Jesus' presence with me I dwell on the most significant of these experiences.

Colloquy

I make expressions of wonder and gratitude at this great mystery that I am the beloved of God. End by saying the *Lord's Prayer*.

PERSONAL REVIEW OF ONE'S EXPERIENCE

I assemble the experiences of my life I wish to share with the other members of the group at this time.

COMMUNAL SHARING

I share with others my prayerful recollection of the special moments of life that have given me the realization that each of us is the beloved of God.

EXERCISE II: OF DESIRES, DREAMS, IDEALS, VISION AND VALUES

Basic to all groups that wish to become discerning communities is the sharing of one's person. The sharing of one's desires, dreams, ideals, vision and values is a good instrument to help people share themselves.

Theme: *Our desires, dreams, ideals, vision and values*

PERSONAL PRAYER

Context

This, then, is what I pray . . . In the abundance of God's glory may God, through the Spirit, enable you to grow firm in power with regard to your inner self, so that Christ may live in your hearts through faith, and then, planted in love and built on love, with all God's holy people you will have the strength to grasp the breadth and the length, the height and the depth; so that knowing the love of Christ, which is beyond knowledge, you may be filled with the utter fullness of God. (Ep 3:14–19)

The grace desired

I seek of God a deep awareness of my basic hopes, dreams, desires and vision of life and the ability to speak about these with the group.

Points

I consider various times in my life when something within me welled up and I was conscious of my deepest hopes and desires for myself and for humanity at large.

I imagine myself with Christ pointing out to me the possibilities in my life and I consider my visions of life.

I reflect on these hopes, dreams, desires and vision to pick out what is most significant for me.

Colloquy

I speak to Christ about my new awareness.

PERSONAL REVIEW OF ONE'S EXPERIENCE

I consider how I will describe these to the other members of our group.

GROUP SHARING

We speak and listen to what each one has found in prayer.

Individually, we reflect after the sharing:
- What impressed me as the others shared?
- Where did I find affective harmony with the others?
- What does this mean for our future?

We share the fruit of this reflection.

NOTES

[1] *A Different Drum* (Simon and Schuster, New York, 1987), p. 58.

[2] John Macmurray: *Religion, Art and Science* (Liverpool University Press, 1961), p. 67: 'We have to distinguish clearly between two types of human unity – a personal type and an impersonal type. The first is a unity of friendship, of fellowship, of community in the full sense . . . The impersonal type . . . is simply a unity of co-operation for a common purpose.' In *Persons in Relation* (Faber and Faber, London, 1961), Macmurray remarks: 'The relations of [a society] are functional . . . A community, however, is a unity of persons as persons. It cannot be defined in functional terms . . . It is constituted and maintained by a mutual affection.'

[3] By 'person' I mean our being, that essential aspect of ourselves that is foundational to the images we have of ourselves and that encloses those aspects of our interior experience that we call ego, superego and self.

[4] Cf. *Treatises on St John*, Tr 17, 7–9.

[5] 'Prayer over the Gifts', *Roman Catholic Sacramentary*, 24th Sunday of the Year.

[6] These last are the expressions used by Gerard W. Hughes in discussing the Ignatian terms 'desolation' and 'consolation' in *God of Surprises* (Darton, Longman and Todd, London, 1985). Something of the range of meaning of these words as used by Ignatius will become clearer as this book proceeds.

2

WHAT IS SPIRITUAL DISCERNMENT?

Test the spirits to see whether they are from God.

(1 Jn 4:1)

I remember a moment when I was trying to discern what the Lord wanted of me in my life. I was a Jesuit novice. As I prayed over my position in the novitiate I was filled with a deep conviction that I had entered the Jesuits because I could not succeed in the world. I was, as Ignatius would have put it, in a state of desolation, that is, 'in darkness of soul and turmoil of spirit' (see Exx 317). I thought I could not stay since I didn't have a vocation. Filled with shame that I would have to leave, I dreaded the loss of the simple, quiet, prayerful life with others that I admired very much. How I wanted to be worthy to stay! I wished I could say to myself that I had been a success in the world and that my vocation was to reject it and to lead a higher life. What was I to do?

Among the scripture passages that the master of novices had given to me for meditative reading was one from St John: 'You did not choose me, no, I chose you' (Jn 15:16). Strangely enough, this filled me with some peace, and I felt able to tell the master of novices that I did not have a vocation since I had entered for the wrong reasons. When I had done this, he asked me how I felt now. Did I want to stay? 'Of course', I said. So he said 'Stay.' We would continue to discern whether I should be a Jesuit.

Looking back I see that there were a number of interior movements in myself at the time. In some way I was forced to face my basic motives for entering the novitiate. I was able to be honest with myself before God. I was given the strength to act upon the truth that I found. Much of this experience was frightening to me. I was full of turmoil and trepidation. I felt alone and bereft of God. But there were also the quiet words of Jesus in John's Gospel. I realize now that I was being called into a genuine experience of humble dependence on God. I moved from an experience of isolation to a sense of union with God. Quiet and peace entered my being. Somehow I knew God would take care of me. So I experienced something of what Ignatius called consolation:

> . . . every increase of faith, hope and love, and all interior joy that invites and attracts to what is heavenly and to the salvation of one's soul by filling it with peace and quiet in its Creator and Lord.

> (Exx 316)

Spiritual discernment is concerned with the movements in the affections and their influence on the interior state of a person and also on his or her actions. As a process, spiritual discernment is a matter of recognizing the initiative of the Holy Spirit so as to follow the Spirit's lead. Sometimes the affective movement is such that discernment moves to decision and action directly and smoothly. At other times careful, even laborious work is necessary for a person to recognize his or her state of being and decide on the action that is appropriate. The basic point of reference in this process of judging the state of one's being is the experience of receiving and giving love unconditionally: in Christian terms, experience of the gracious (grace-giving) God.

Spiritual discernment is a skill, which has to be learned and practised. St Paul names discernment of spirits among the gifts of the Holy Spirit, but even those who are specially gifted for it need to exercise their gift constantly. For others it is an acquired skill, which can develop into an art.

Individual discernment, moreover, is not complete unless it considers the experience of Christianity and humanity. There is no individual discernment outside a communal setting and no communal discernment without individual discernment. Each individual profits from the communal activity of discernment and the community profits from each individual's discernment. The community shares the gifts of the members – their wisdom, faithfulness, joy, patience, compassion, truthfulness and gentleness, as well as their discernment. This is true of the church as a whole, as well as of communities, small or great, within it, as indeed it is ultimately true of any society.

26

Purposes of discernment

There are three notable purposes of spiritual discernment. The first is enhancement of self-knowledge and well-being. This is the product of much prayerful reflection upon oneself. One becomes aware of interior movements and their significance, getting in touch with motivations that might otherwise remain in the unconscious.

Second, through spiritual discernment we learn greater appreciation of the presence and activity of God in us and our universe. This is important for one's interior state of being for it heightens awareness of the presence of God in our intimate experiences with God. It also heightens awareness of forces for good and evil acting upon us.

A third purpose of spiritual discernment, and the natural flowering of the other two, is to enable our free response in decision and action to the Spirit of God moving us forward to fulfil our ultimate purpose and desire: to be instruments of God's oneness, beauty, truth and goodness in our world, that is, to be one with Christ in serving both God and humanity. This brings us into a fuller sense of ourselves as active agents in our world. 'For we are God's work of art, created in Christ Jesus for the good works which God has already designated to make up our way of life' (Ep 2:10). In a sense, discernment is a truncated experience if it does not include response in action. When it moves to this purpose discernment becomes a spirituality of choice leading to action. Then the interrelationship of discernment and action can be appreciated. The interior activity of choosing becomes linked to the realm of external action.

The perspective of faith

In this book we are concerned with spiritual discernment in the context of Christian faith, in which the meaning of life is to be found in the life, death and resurrection of Jesus Christ. In this faith perspective, not just particular experiences but one's whole life, or even the life of the human race can be the matter for discernment. Individuals or communities examining their lives with the eyes of faith see all the events of their lives as their personal or communal faith history, or graced history. They include painful and joyful events, sinful and redemptive, times when they perceive themselves to have responded to God's call, and times when they failed to respond.

Today, through modern psychology, we appreciate the influence of our historical experience on our responses and reactions to life as we live it. In fact, we suspect that the long line of our ancestry back to the first parents of the human race is present in our memories and genetic code. So we realize that much recall and analysis of the hidden unconscious is important if we are to understand interior experiences and motivations. Through patiently listening to people and helping them analyse their dreams psychologists can surface much unconscious material.

Christians are able to accept some of these insights of psychology, but view them from the perspective of faith. The hidden unconscious contains two sets of memory experiences going back into the distant past. One set might be considered as the presence of God calling and moving this long line of human experience forward to the fullness of human development as a divine–human community in Christ. The other set might be considered as the non-response of humans to the call of God. Knowledge of such historical experience is significant. Of course, it is humanly impossible to know one's entire history and recall it for discernment and action, and an attempt to do so can lead to a narcissistic fascination with the unconscious, to scrupulosity and inaction.

Christian discernment is balanced by awareness of immediate experiences of the felt presence or absence of God and the ability to know their meaning in terms of our response. These are religious experiences of good and of evil, our own immediate peak religious experiences of spiritual consolation and spiritual desolation. They need to be reflected upon and appropriated as further criteria for interpreting our interior life and motivations.

A third set of experiences requiring a form of discernment impinges on us from the social context in which we live. Recognizing and knowing the significance of this set of experiences involves a type of reflection usually named 'reading the signs of the times' or 'doing social analysis' or answering the question: 'What does it mean to love the neighbour?'

28

THE DYNAMIC OF DISCERNMENT

The wisdom of Ignatius

The psychology and, in some ways, the theological language of Ignatius' day was very different from our own. His great insight was into the importance of considering not just our interior moods, feelings or affections, but their tendency or direction, whether their end is such that the person knows that he or she is being drawn Godwards or away from God. Ignatius expresses this in the language of his time in terms of good or bad spirits or angels operating from within or beyond the person, and so speaks of movement of spirits, and discernment of spirits. We here use his language because a better one has not so far been developed; but in this book we are concerned with the value of his insight for the life and growth of small Christian communities, not in defending the details of its expression.

Ignatius also recognized experiences that do not need discernment, that are not describable in terms of movement of spirits. He speaks of the experience of God acting directly on the person, giving the experience he calls 'consolation without previous cause'. He describes this as the self-evident experience of unconditional love. We can include here awareness of God's love coming through all the universe. A sense of harmony with the life forces of our planet will be included in the affective awareness of God's unconditional love for the human race experienced by the individual at such a moment.

The process of discernment

I usually approach the dynamic of discernment as a five-phase process, including *experience, reflection, articulation, interpretation* and *decision-and-action*. The whole of the process has to be kept in mind. Every one of the five phases is important and each phase interacts with the others. It is often difficult to recognize where one phase

29

begins and another lets off. The process is cyclical and the cycles can happen very quickly.

It is helpful also to remember that this is a heuristic process, that is, one of ongoing discovery. One never grasps the fullness of one's life. The memory is that faculty of our being that keeps revealing the significance of God's constant presence, if we have the disposition to receive its messages. We can assist the memory by recalling events of our lives.

Now let us look at how discernment of spirits can be understood in terms of this five-phase dynamic as it applies to individuals.

EXPERIENCE

Experience is the starting point of spiritual discernment. All of our experience is important because there God's presence is recognized. This implies a theology that acknowledges the significance of human endeavour in the eyes of God.

The subject matter for discernment may be the totality of people's life experience. They will ask the questions that faith prompts: 'Why did God arrange that I be born in *this* place of *this* sort of family?' 'What is God's view of my successes and failures?' 'How was God calling me in this and that event?' 'In what ways have I refused God's call?'[1]

In other instances people will focus on particular experiences. If they come to look on these as religious experiences, they will want to test their authenticity, and whether they indicate a special call from God at this moment in their lives. Sometimes these experiences are extraordinary. St Ignatius describes one such in his autobiography: 'One day . . . his understanding was raised on high, so as to see the Most Holy Trinity under the aspect of three keys on a musical instrument, and as a result he shed many tears and sobbed so strongly that he could not control himself.'[2] At other times they are the stuff of everyday life.

REFLECTION

Reflecting on what has taken place throughout the period being examined is the second phase. It is the first attempt at understanding the movement of spirits in one's interior. Briefly, the person is examining the way he or she is moving or being moved in relation to other persons in terms of the love of God. The person questions if he or she is being drawn in love from God or whether he or she is turning in on self.

People may reflect actively, questioning themselves about their life stories or the part of their life under consideration; or they may reflect passively, 'staying with it' until they find meaning or a sense of God's presence in their life. In all kinds of ways they will be able to recognize the presence of God in incidents of suffering and failure as well as in joyful situations, since often some incident in their past life that was avoided as too painful emerges as an occasion for growing in relationship with others and God. The break-up of a love affair, failure at school or work, natural tragedies, and dysfunctional family situations may come to be seen as occasions for changing the course of life.

Persons who are reflecting on a single incident of life or a recent experience of prayer will be looking for a more affective knowledge of God. Such incidents can bring about a type of conversion for they may throw light on all their other life experiences. This happens when people are given a deep experience of God's love for them. Conversion experiences may also bring about a new way of facing the future.

The reflection proposed here involves a further awareness of the effectiveness of the love of God in these experiences. People ask whether they are being moved by the love of God. Are they being drawn beyond themselves or turned in on themselves? The experience of being drawn beyond themselves by love from God results in an expansive, open attitude to all humanity and to God. The experience of turning in on oneself results in a pleasurable or painful sense of aloneness. It is possible to recognize and reflect on the movements contained in such experiences with some degree of detachment even though they may be affecting the person on a feeling and intimate level.

To accomplish this review may take some time for often we do not recognize what have been our interior experiences and which forces are at work in us. It is important to seek light from the Holy Spirit. Continually writing down such reviews can be a good way to begin a spiritual journal. This review is the basis of the next phase, articulation.

ARTICULATION

Articulation is significant for several reasons. First, it places people in a communal context. Second, it helps the person to become more objective in her or his understanding of the experience examined. Third, it may be the occasion for new insights for the person speaking and for those listening. Fourth, it is part of the forward experience of discernment.

With this phase people attempt to express what happened to them from a Christian perspective and in terms of a theology that accepts the activity of spiritual forces from within and from beyond one's being. Individually such expression can be done by writing in a spiritual journal or reporting to another person. In a community it takes place when persons share the fruit of reflection on their life experiences, including formal prayer experiences.

Sometimes the community has to listen very intently to catch the movement being expressed. Persons who are recounting elements of their own history will usually focus on one incident that helped them to understand many other aspects of their life. They often begin by describing the incident in a factual way, e.g. 'After high school I went immediately into university. My friends were hitchhiking around Europe and Asia. Now I think such experience would have made university a more fruitful time in my life.' Or, 'It was during World War II and I had just failed my second year at university and so I joined the Air Force. It looked like two years wasted. I've always felt that I should have joined up after high school.' Then they proceed to describe the affective state of their being as they realized how the years were not wasted but a time for maturity and facing the significance of creaturehood before God. Eventually they describe an affective experience of awareness of God's presence to them throughout this history, a sense of wholeness in place of fragmentation, and the accompanying desire to be an instrument of God's presence and goodness to others.

Similarly, the community may have to wait a while to recognize the significance of someone's prayer experience. The person may begin by recounting the matter of her or his prayer: 'It was 4:30 in the afternoon. I was contemplating Matthew's account of the baptism of Jesus at the Jordan. All at once I was in the water with Jesus.' Then the person will describe what happened to them in their hearts. 'I felt such a sinner. Why was I in the water with Jesus? But Jesus embraced me. The next thing I sensed was Jesus embracing all those I had offended and all who had sinned against me.'

Members of the community may realize that they have had similar experiences. They can support the person sharing by saying so or interacting with the one sharing in order to draw out the deeper significance of the incident being shared.

Language is important at such a time. Those listening to the stories will recognize some of the experience. They will be able to question the speakers to help them recognize the spiritual element in their experience. In the interchange they can help them interpret the experience and its implications for the future. They may suspect that some of their experiences are not from the Spirit but have a destructive tendency, although generally those who listen should be 'more ready to give a good interpretation of the statement of another than to condemn' (Exx 22).

INTERPRETATION

This is the formal moment of discernment. It is the activity by which persons realize the significance of the interior movement of spirits. In a community this takes place during the interchange after a member has reviewed his or her life since the last meeting. Members will question the speaker and try to decide whether the experience was one of spiritual consolation or one of spiritual desolation. Then they will search out with the speaker the meaning of the consolation or the desolation.

The words consolation and desolation are used to describe the two understandings of one's being and the attendant movements of love or lack of love as described by Ignatius (Exx 316, 317). In determining whether the experience is spiritual consolation or spiritual desolation it is important to realize that it is the *movement* in the experience that is the matter for discernment. So a painful sense of self (sorrow, mourning, compassion for another's suffering) can be a consolation because one is moving beyond oneself. And a feeling of pleasure (such as overweening pride of self) can be a desolation. An outside listener with distance from the immediate experience can often recognize the movement in the experience and name it as consolation or desolation more easily than the person who had the experience.

Consolation and desolation are not good or bad in themselves although we tend to desire and pray for consolations. They are basically interior experiences. The further discernment of the meaning of the experiences for the person's present state of being or for future decision and action is highly significant. Sometimes a person is given an experience of spiritual consolation to assist the image of self, or to give the person energy to carry on as a disciple of the Lord. Sometimes a person is given desolation to assist the person to realize all is gift or to show that a proposed course of action is not in tune with the person's basic well-being with God and as such is not a true movement. Recognizing the meaning in the interior movements usually indicates some future attitude or actions. It is the time of energy and encouragement and commitment to following the lead of the Spirit into the future.

In a community where the members know each other's history they will make connections with the speaker's whole life history. They will seek to name the movement and discover its meaning for future action. Knowing the person's history can help the members recognize whether a consoling experience is really a deception under the guise of light, goodness or superficial love (cf. Exx 332–4). When it is not clear, the community will encourage the speaker to go back and reflect some more on the event. If it is truly consolation the speaker will recognize the connection with the faith-meaning of her or his history and be strengthened to be open and face life in peace and joy in God. The one praying will have an energized hope for the future. The community can now help the speaker consider the meaning of the experience for present and future decisions and actions.

DECISION-AND-ACTION: FOLLOWING THE LEAD OF THE
SPIRIT

Decision and action necessarily follow the interpretation of the
movement of spirits. If they do not, the previous phases are a sham.
In fact if some consideration of the implications for future decisions
and actions is not taken into account during the phase of articulation, it is questionable if the interpretation will be correct. With
the fifth phase the person considers how he or she will fulfil the call
of the spirit that has been discerned. Again it is helpful to discuss
the proposed concrete attitude or action with the community. This
is the moment of response to the call the person has discerned in
the other four phases, the time when reflection moves to action.

For persons whose discernment has been over their personal
graced history this phase may bring them to decisions regarding
their life-style: their way of relating to the environment, relationship
with the faith community, daily prayer practice and ministry to
others. I think of people who make it a practice to examine themselves each day to discover how 'God has shown his face to them'.
They may come to realize, for instance, that they can now practise
a more wholesome way of eating and drinking. They may cut
back on entertainment and sport so that concern for the poor and
almsgiving become priorities.

It is similar with those whose discernment has been over special
religious experiences. Even before this phase, e.g., in a prayer
experience with Jesus at his baptism, let us say that someone may
have surmised that this is suggesting a missionary life. Then she or
he may become frightened of the implications of their prayer and
be challenged in freedom. Now they will take this possible action
to prayer and decide through a discernment of spirits whether God
is calling them to this action. The affective knowledge of the presence of God to them gained in the interpreting phase assists them
in discerning the desires of God regarding this future possibility of
becoming a missionary.

The cycle continued as a way of life

The experience of action introduces a new cycle of the five phases, and continual use of this five-phase cycle develops the spirituality of discernment as a way of life. A great help to this way of life is the continual use of any one of the various 'awareness exercises'. Most of these follow Ignatius' process of thanksgiving, prayer for light, examining one's day, responding to what is found in sorrow or joy, and praying to be more responsive to grace in the future. The five phases of discernment are present in these various activities of the awareness exercise.[3]

An example of communal discernment

Some years ago I was with a Christian community of eleven lay persons going through a discernment process. For many years this community had enjoyed a certain recognition in the area as a central group for prayer and for their compassionate concern for the handicapped as well as a rallying point for those suffering from unjust situations. The community was beginning to experience some rejection from persons of note in the larger community. It was for this reason that they asked themselves how they might continue to live the communal life-style they valued so much.

They followed a process similar to the five phases presented above. At the start they developed a history line, that is, they looked at the whole history of their community to facilitate reflection on the way they had come together and on what had happened to them through their eight years of shared life.

Then they reflected individually over their communal history, seeking to get in touch with and appreciate the way God had been with them. They looked for interior movements of consolation, desolation and spiritual understanding in their prayer.

After this they shared what they were given in prayer. At this time there were enhanced communal experiences of consolation and desolation. Also during this sharing they expressed basic hurts and anger caused by church structures and those in authority. The sharing included an acknowledgement of their own disorders and sinfulness. A type of interior reconciliation then took place among themselves and with the church and civic community to which they belonged.

As they considered their communal history from a spiritual viewpoint they recognized certain communal desolations such as being isolated from other Christians and people in the city in their attempt to live a simple life dedicated to developing just structures. They recalled many instances of communal consolation: unity and energy among themselves and realizations that they had been instruments of God's truth, compassion and encouragement to others suffering from unjust structures.

When they looked to their future they realized that they needed someone objective to help them discern some of their basic decisions and actions. The community proceeded to gather possible answers to their need and focused on joining a larger organization that was promoting the same ideals and values as they had. As they prayed with this possibility many fears and concerns surfaced: an added financial burden, getting locked into a bureaucratic structure that could destroy their own free discernment process, and new responsibilities as officers of the larger organization. But they also had increased experiences of energy and hope as they recognized the similar values and processes present in the larger organization. In their discernment they felt that the best way for them to gain some objectivity in their communal decisions and actions was with the larger organization. They knew that all would not be rosy and that burdens would be placed on them but they felt that God was calling them to take the step of joining this organization. They applied for membership in the organization with conviction that this was congruent with their past communal history. They committed themselves in faith and hope to this continual development.

The two processes: individual and communal discernment

There are similarities and differences between individual and communal discernment. Except that the subject is the community and the context is communal, the three purposes of discernment are the same: communal well-being and self knowledge, awareness of the felt presence of God to the community, and communal response to the Spirit of God moving the group forward. The five-phase process also applies in both cases, as well as private prayer and public disclosure as the discernment goes on.

In individual discernment, however, although there is some disclosure about one's interior movement of spirits, the actual discernment is a private affair. This does not mean that there is no communal dimension in the individual's discernment, but it is private rather than public. The individual seeks to recognize the kind of experience taking place and to grasp the meaning of the consolations and desolations so he or she can follow the lead of the Spirit.

The importance of story is rather different in the two kinds of discernment. In-depth awareness of one's story (personal graced history) is helpful in assisting a person to interpret present prayer experiences; but story is especially significant for community. The communal graced history needs to be recalled and expressed often for the sake of establishing community itself and for a discernment of communal call or deception.

More time is given to public activity in communal discernment. In individual discernment the main activity is the private prayer of the person, while in communal discernment the main activity is the public interrelationship. In individual discernment the public activity occurs during the steps of articulation and interpretation. It is during these steps that the individual attempts to express and interpret what was experienced in private prayer. Other persons can be of great help in the interpretation. During this interchange the one discerning is relating to the faith community and the person guiding the community.

In communal discernment, on the other hand, there are times of private prayer and reflection but the bulk of time and activity is in the public sphere. The public time of the group is the basis for private reflection and communal discernment. For example, when a group prays over its communal graced history some time is given to private prayer, but discussion of the material for prayer that precedes the private prayer and the sharing of the results of that prayer take much more time. Time is also necessary for understanding the significance of the community's experiences in terms of consolation and desolation and for subsequent decision-making.

Discernment as guarantee of authentic Christian community

Some people are critical of the various forms of small groups that assemble for faith-sharing. They are concerned that these groups only come together for their own sake. They watch such groups appearing to be self-centred and even self-righteous in relationship with others. They sense that some of these Christian groups exclude others, almost like clubs.

Such judgements may not be totally justified. The purpose and image of a group has to be considered. There are various kinds of groups and not all are the result of interpersonal commitment to each other or to others beyond the group. Some are basically support groups or therapeutic groups. As such they tend, quite legitimately, to focus on themselves. Other groups have concerns and act beyond themselves. They may be Christian task forces or action groups.

A group which desires to be a committed community for the betterment of humanity will find the discernment process very helpful in its growth and apostolic decisions. If it images itself as a community of disciples in the Lord, or as a faith community called to bring gospel values to humanity, then its reflections on experience, its articulations and interpretations will be such that it will be open to the Spirit calling it beyond itself for the good of others.

Such groups will find the five-phase process of discernment helpful in overcoming some of the pitfalls of communal life. This process will be an instrument of God's grace, helping it to use the shared wisdom of its members and to benefit from past experiences and focus its future hopes and desires. Thus it becomes a more effective instrument for God's grace in the world.

Communal spiritual discernment presumes that there is a uniqueness about the community that comes from the makeup of its membership and the events it has experienced together. The community needs to discover this uniqueness. This means that the community gets in touch with its own unique experiences, both those that it recognizes as coming from or pointing to God, and also those that draw it away from God.

In trying further to grasp the meaning of such experiences in terms of a movement to God or away from God, the community intends to follow the direction of call from God that it recognizes, or at least to move away from patterns of experience that it considers destructive to itself or those beyond it.

The fifth phase of this discerning process is capable of drawing a group beyond itself provided that persons honestly give themselves to the other four phases. For the fifth phase is concerned with the significance of the experience, reflection, articulation and interpretation for decision. It is true that sometimes significant decisions and actions may revolve around the inner workings of the community to make it more loving and open within itself, but it also senses itself being called to perform acts of love to those beyond it such as the community of Macedonia performed for the Christians of Jerusalem (2 Co 8:1–5). If action for persons beyond the group does not ultimately happen, there is probably a wrong interpretation of the significance of the experience that has been reflected upon and articulated in the group: a Christian community is called to include everyone in its love and concern.

This means that the fifth phase of discerned decisions makes communal discernment a communal spirituality of action. The group then becomes a cell of the church, bringing gospel service to the whole of humanity. The group might image itself as a community of disciples of the Lord or stewards of the gifts of God.

Coda: the place of a spiritual guide in discernment

A spiritual guide is helpful in both individual and communal discernment. But the role and activity of the guide are quite different; this shows up in the various private and public elements in the two situations.

Individual discernment is done from the individual's interior experience. The spiritual guide assists the individual to discern interior movements and their significance for individual decisions and actions. Because the individual is doing the discernment a spiritual guide only needs a limited amount of information to help the individual.

The spiritual guide of a community needs a greater amount of detail from the group concerning its history and its interrelationships to assist the group to discern. It will be helpful if the guide is present to assist the group to pray about and share its communal graced history. This activity is helpful to the guide because it reveals much of the community to him or her and establishes the public nature of communal discernment. This allows the spiritual guide to interpret the meaning of the various external interchanges that take place as the members speak and listen to each other.

In personal spiritual direction disclosure is necessary to assist the individual to understand her or his own interior motivations and calls from the Lord. While this applies to the interior life of a community also, a further purpose of disclosure is actually to bring about community and help it develop and grow.

EXERCISE III: TO HELP PERSONS APPRECIATE THE MOVEMENT OF SPIRITS IN THEIR LIVES

In discerning communities all the members desire to follow the lead of the Spirit. They are willing to discern and reflect on interior and exterior movement of spirits. They will do the two discernments, individual and communal, and they are willing to disclose their interior life to each other. An exercise on one's personal graced history can be a good way to begin these practices.

Theme: Personal graced history

PERSONAL PRAYER

Context

Yes, I know what plans I have in mind for you, Yahweh declares, plans for peace, not for disaster, to give you a future and a hope. When you call to me and come and pray to me, I shall listen to you. When you search for me, you will find me; when you search wholeheartedly for me, I shall let you find me. (Jr 29:11–14)

The grace desired

I seek the grace to be present to my life history as it is lovingly told by God, and I pray that I may respond more generously to the love of God flooding my heart.

Considerations

I enter into my own sense of creaturehood, of freedom, of being a sinner, of call to build the kingdom with the Lord, of light from the Lord, of suffering with the Lord and of joy in the Lord.

I look over my life story searching out those special times where I have experienced the presence of the Lord in these ways.

I enter into the ones that most impress me at this time.

Colloquy

I speak to the Lord, in various ways expressing my appreciation and gratitude for God's presence to me in my life. I close with the *Lord's Prayer*.

PERSONAL REVIEW OF ONE'S EXPERIENCE

I assemble the experiences of my life I wish to share with the other members of the group at this time.

GROUP SHARING

This consists of listening to the others as they express the results of their prayer, reflecting on the sharing, and then briefly expressing the significance of the sharing for each member of the group.

Share

I express to the others those moments of my graced history that I have returned to: the joyful and light ones, the sorrowful and dark ones, the glorious and hope-filled ones.

I listen intently to the experiences of the others.

Reflection on the sharing

I pause for about five minutes and reflect on what impressed me as the others shared their graced history.

Further sharing

I share these impressions with the other members of the group.

Notes: 1. Ways of praying with graced history

Pray over this history in all the ways you would pray with sacred scripture.

CONTEMPLATE

Re-live the event by seeing the persons, hearing the words, observing the actions.

LECTIO DIVINA

Regard an event of your history as sacred scripture spoken by God in your life personally or communally. Read this word by remembering the event with all your senses. Ponder the event by searching out the meaning of it. Realize God's presence in it. Respond to it with acts of awe, wonder, gratitude, resolve and self-offering.

MEDITATE

Question the Lord about the events of this history and seek its meaning.

QUIET PRAYER

Take one moment of this history as an experience of God's presence to you and abide with it as it resides in the depths of your being. Use whichever method(s) you are most comfortable with.

REVIEW OF PRAYER

Spend some time reflecting on what happened to you in this time of prayer.

2. Sharing the results of prayer in small groups

The prime purpose of group sharing is to listen to each other. We are not a study group or a discussion group, so we do not make judgements on each other's responses. Our purpose is to obtain a communal sense of the group's graced history by listening to what the other members of the group have found in their reflection over the group's graced history.

After reflecting on what was given in prayer, each member shares in a brief way what impressed her or him. No one member should dominate the group's time. The emphasis should be on listening to and absorbing what has been said; only then does someone speak.

NOTES

[1] In the book *Choosing Life* (Paulist, New York, 1979), I do a fairly extensive treatment of the subject of discovering that one's whole life history is an experience of grace. Approaching life as a graced experience enables a person to discover the qualities of his or her unique spiritual consolation.
[2] Cf. Joseph N. Tylenda SJ (trans.): *A Pilgrim's Journey, the Autobiography of Ignatius Loyola* (Michael Glazier, Wilmington, Delaware, 1985), p. 36; or William Yeomans SJ (trans.): *Inigo: Original Testament* (Inigo Enterprises, London, 1985).
[3] Cf. Exx 43 and recent explanations by George Aschenbrenner SJ: 'Con-

sciousness Examen', in *Review for Religious* (Vol. 31, #1, 1972), pp. 14–21; and John Govan sj: 'The Examen: A Tool for Holistic Growth', in *Review for Religious* (Vol.45, #3, 1986), pp. 394–401.

THE SECRET OF COMMUNAL DISCERNMENT: RECOGNIZING SPIRITUAL CONSOLATION

For . . . in consolation the good spirit guides and counsels us.
(Ignatius Loyola, Spiritual Exercises 318)

I once accompanied a group through a decision-making process in which they prayed individually over their communal history and shared the interior movements and insights experienced in prayer. As the group recounted its history it became obvious that suffering was a dominant dimension. An image gradually surfaced to express this suffering. They sensed that they were like a rejected step-child in a family. The image expressed their historical experience of insignificance and being set aside as a smaller group within a larger institution which had different priorities and concerns. They even felt that they were only tolerated because their apostolic work was a source of income for the larger institution. As the group worked with this image its sense of desolation seemed to grow in terms of anger, helplessness and hopelessness. This lasted for a number of sessions.

Gradually, another realization came to them: an awareness that they were indeed instruments of God's truth and goodness right in the midst of this pain of being a rejected step-child. They recalled that people had even affirmed the group as an example of co-operative team spirit encouraging others in faith, hope and love. Yet they tended only to experience themselves as disunited, confused, broken and rejected.

Although the rejected step-child image recalled some very painful moments in the group's history, they found it spiritually consoling. There was little desire to have such experiences again. Yet they were able to return to their painful experience and use it as a criterion for judging their state of being as they made decisions about themselves as a community.

The discovery and articulation of the image of rejected step-child was a spiritual consolation because it helped them to find God in their experience and freed them to make tough decisions for the future. This spiritual consolation was present to them in their difficult decision and as a confirmation of it. The group had come to realize that their identity as a group included this painful historical experience. They were given the spiritual understanding that this was an experience of living Jesus' words: 'If any want to become my followers, let them renounce themselves and take up their cross and follow me. For those who . . . lose their life for my sake, and for the sake of the gospel, will save it' (Mk 8:34, 35). When the group came to the moment of decision they were faced with possible cost to themselves if the proposal went into act. They met this challenge in terms of St Paul's experience and prayer:

> . . . so that I should not get above myself, I was given a thorn in the flesh . . . About this, I have three times pleaded with the Lord that it might leave me, but he has answered me, 'My grace is enough for you: for power is at full stretch in weakness.' It is, then, about my weaknesses that I am happiest of all to boast, so that the power of Christ may rest upon me . . . For it is when I am weak that I am strong.
>
> (2 Co 12:7–10)

> [I want to know Christ] and the power of his resurrection, and partake of his sufferings by being moulded to the pattern of his death.
>
> (Ph 3:10)

The group now began to view the image of themselves as a step-child in a new light. They became conscious that this is the way the realm of God happens. They were filled with the consolation of being with Christ, the rejected cornerstone, and opened themselves up to future experiences of being step-child with a certain trepidation but hope.

Communal discernment

Discernment in a small faith community begins with the recognition that God's Spirit is at work in us, motivating us to live as Jesus did. It acknowledges our human freedom and responsibility. We realize that we are called and can do something for ourselves and all humanity. We are drawn out of isolated positions as individuals and so gain hope and energy. The church's memory of its long history underpins the group's own individual and shared memories. Eventually, communal discernment gives a group a sense of its own unique identity, in which the significance of every member is acknowledged, their presence to the group as well as their particular gifts.

Because the discernment occurs through shared insights and affections a certain level of affectionate relationship among the members of a group and between the group and Christ develops. This brings about an atmosphere of trust, freedom and willingness to risk. Since discernment aims at decisions at the level of faith, freedom with all sides of an issue is also necessary. It gradually builds.

As the group faces the reality of its limitedness and sinfulness a new sense of trust and fellowship takes place. Reconciliation is possible and the group opens up to call and mission.

The heart of discernment: spiritual consolation

Discernment is basically the activity of becoming aware of one's motivations from a faith perspective. It is a judgement about the affective awareness of interpersonal relationships in terms of God's call. For a Christian this intimate knowledge eventually focuses on the personal and affective awareness of the person of Christ that is attained through contemplation, whether this contemplation is on the mysteries of Christ's life as presented in the gospels or on the mystery of one's own graced life. Actually in contemplation these two aspects of mystery interact, the gospel message giving insight into my own life and my life giving insight into the gospel. The coming together of the gospel mystery with my own life may result in an experience of spiritual consolation. For example, I may have

48

read about and used my imagination with the disciples on the way to Emmaus in Luke and recalled Jesus' words that it was 'necessary that the Christ should suffer before entering into his glory' (Lk 24:26) and believe that this is true. Yet I do not have intimate knowledge of this truth of the faith. But if I bring my own life into the contemplation and experience how Christ has brought life out of death for me, or energy out of despondency, or hope in the face of fear, then I will be given the spiritual consolation of intimate knowledge of this truth and intimate knowledge of Jesus.

Much of St Ignatius' *Spiritual Exercises* is designed to help people identify and focus on experiences of spiritual consolation. He has a very positive attitude to life and sees God as benevolent and supportive of human beings.

> It is characteristic of God and the good spirits, when they act upon the soul, to give true happiness and spiritual joy, and to banish all the sadness and disturbances caused by the enemy. It is characteristic of the evil one to fight against such happiness and spiritual consolation by suggesting false reasonings, subtleties, and continual deceptions.
>
> (Exx 329)

But we are aware that many of the well beloved of God (Christ and the saints) seem to have gone through excruciating experiences of pain and darkness interiorly as well as exteriorly. So the terms 'happiness', 'joy', 'sadness' and 'disturbances' must have special connotations for Ignatius. Here are his own words:

> I call it consolation when the soul is aroused by an interior movement which causes it to be inflamed with love for its Creator and Lord, and as a consequence can love no created thing on the face of the earth for its own sake, but only in the Creator of all things. It is likewise consolation when one sheds tears, moved by love for God, whether it be because of sorrow for sins, or because of the sufferings of Christ our Lord, or for any other reason immediately directed to the service and praise of God. Finally I call consolation every increase of faith, hope and love, and all interior joy which calls and attracts the soul to that which is of God and to salvation by filling it with tranquillity and peace in its Creator and Lord.
>
> (Exx 316)

I call desolation that which is entirely the opposite of what was described in the third rule, such as darkness of soul, confusion of spirit, attraction to what is base and worldly, restlessness caused by many disturbances and temptations which lead to lack of faith, hope, or love. The soul finds itself completely apathetic, lukewarm, sad and as if separated from its Creator and Lord. For just as consolation is the opposite of desolation, so the thoughts coming from consolation are the opposite of those which come from desolation.

(Exx 317)

Ignatius is speaking about motivations or affective motions or interior movements in one's being.[1] The significant aspect in his description of consolation and desolation is the movement, regardless of whether the feeling is painful or pleasurable. Spiritual consolation then is an interior experience of the movement of the affections outward to other human persons, the whole of humanity, to the communion of saints, Christ and the Trinity, painful as that might be at times. Spiritual desolation is an interior experience of movement of the affections into oneself alone, pleasurable as that might be at times.[2]

Even in painful experiences of consolation we have to remember that the affective experience of spiritual consolation still has a sweetness to it although sometimes it is a bitter sweetness, and desolation ultimately has an emptiness, although it may be quite pleasurable.

Spiritual consolation is different from the experiences we ordinarily call consolation. There are hard and easy spiritual consolations. The painful effort of someone's defending truth, justice, peace or honesty at all costs is an experience of spiritual consolation if the person senses 'God is with me in this.' It is helpful to note that Ignatius includes experiences of sorrow under consolation. Spiritual consolation includes all those interior movements of being that draw the person to the One, the Beautiful, the True, the Good.

Is communal spiritual consolation possible?

Spiritual discernment involves getting in touch with one's interior movements or motivations and judging whether these are coming from the Holy Spirit or from self-indulgence. Can we really speak about communal spiritual discernment?

Some people would say that communal spiritual discernment is only good group dynamics; or that it is the sum-total of everyone's private discernment. Others would agree that a community can practise spiritual discernment, but they would want to qualify the experience of spiritual consolation. They would admit that a community can have an experience of peace and unity when good group process is taking place. For during such a process satisfaction is experienced because all members feel they have been heard, all issues have been addressed, the sufferings to be undergone have been faced. There is a sense that the members of the group have entered into the process freely, without holding anything back, and have given themselves to it in terms of Christian principles. There can be a sense of Christian unity and peace among the group.

There are accounts of communal religious experience in scripture. We think especially of the resurrection appearances of Jesus in the Christian Testament. In the Hebrew Testament many religious experiences are attested to by all the people, for example, the covenant experience of Moses and the Israelites on Mount Sinai in Exodus 19:16–25.

But can we say that a community as a community can have and recognize a communal experience of spiritual consolation? In answer, I would like to present an experience which I judge to be communal spiritual consolation and then indicate to you how the community returned to this experience in communal discernment.[3]

During a workshop on communal discernment I asked a community of religious women (about seventy members, sixty per cent over fifty years of age) to recall some communal activities and reflect on one in which they sensed that they had experienced communal spiritual consolation.

The occasion which they selected was the death of two of their young sisters in an automobile accident five years earlier and the funeral which followed this tragedy.

The experience they described included the state of shock that the community was in for the following two days. Yet people reported a sense that something beautiful and good was happening to them as a community during the day of the funeral. They returned to the experience in order to describe it in terms of feelings, images, concepts and phrases.

The feelings that the community experienced during the two days were described in these ways: disbelief in its reality ('It couldn't happen to us'), anger with the superiority of God ('Is God really with us?'), being shaken to the core, a stupefying effect, disintegration, doubting, 'equalizing of people', emptiness, powerlessness, unspeakable sorrow, grieving, forgiveness of others, new openness to persons not part of the community.

The feelings that something beautiful and good was happening to them as a community, especially during the day of the funeral, were described as communion in pain, communal loss, communion in humility, communion with people outside their immediate religious community – with the blood families, the city, other religious orders and even the nation. The funeral itself was a bittersweet experience. There was great mourning and yet a sense of being loved and cared for as a community. They experienced a new kind of unity and belonging. They had a new awareness of the love and presence of God to them as a community. They could even recognize the suffering Christ in their midst and identify his presence in their community.

The images that remained with them were: people hugging and crying, people in hushed groups, many lay people in the hallways, broken families of the sisters gathered in the community house, the community itself as a family face to face with death, receiving from others, open to others, two caskets in the church for a long time, an endless procession, two young sisters sobbing through the funeral, the gathering of themselves into community through the homily and liturgy of the funeral.

The phrases and concepts that were now present in recall were unity, poverty, dependence, peace through pain, hope, trust. 'The Lord is close to the broken-hearted.' 'The best of ourselves came out.' 'You could ask anybody to do anything.' Re-gathering, reunion, reconciliation, Micah's words: 'Act justly . . . love tenderly . . . walk humbly with your God.' 'God is directing and carrying us.' 'In our weakness is our strength.'

Upon reflection they got more in touch with what had been given to them as a community. They recounted something else that is quite extraordinary, a true expression of the larger faith community we call church. The religious women themselves were in a great state of shock and practically incapable of organizing the funeral and reception which would ordinarily follow a funeral of one of their members. Their lay friends took over. They moved in and took care of the reception desk, the funeral arrangements, the announcements and invitations. Later they prepared the residence for the funeral mass and reception. They organized the music and prepared the reception hall and the meal. They gathered in great numbers to be with the sisters to celebrate the entrance into glory of their deceased sisters.

The capacity to recognize communal spiritual consolation becomes particularly important in the ongoing life of a community when it is in the process of serious decision-making. After the funeral the community of sisters judged that the experience was one of communal spiritual consolation and as such was significant in their ongoing communal discernment. So they proceeded to interpret its meaning for them and later they returned to it as they made communal decisions.

1. NEW AWARENESS

The experience had given the group a new sense of who it was – a new identity – especially in relationship to the larger church. They viewed themselves in a new light. Previously they saw themselves as serving the larger community. Now they became conscious of how the larger community had served them. The experience affected the community's aspirations, desires, vision and planning. Certain elements are easily recognized in their experience.

1) A significant factor in this communal experience was the human element: a particular event in time and place. It was an expression of human compassion, love, kindness and strength.

2) The experience was communal, especially the funeral.

3) The experience carried with it much communal affection.

4) The sisters felt a sense of awe, as well as humility, at the surprising way the Lord, through the lay community, had taken over in this time of distress.

5) They acknowledged an outpouring of love from others not belonging to their immediate group.

6) They themselves had a new sense of unity and belonging.

7) They sensed the presence of Christ and his paschal mystery in a new way and so they were given a new dimension of faith, hope, love.

8) They experienced a new peace and energy.

9) They experienced a new sense of identity, vocation, mission and celebration.

2. LATER INFLUENCES OF THIS EXPERIENCE

The phrase, 'In our weakness is our strength', became significant in the decisions which flowed immediately from the experience and also in decisions made later. This time of consolation became a point of reference for future discernment.

Impact on immediate decisions: Following this experience of being loved by the larger faith community they realized that they had to search for and rediscover the basic spirituality that energized them as an apostolic community. Recognizing and appreciating the communal presence of Christ in human interchange became an important element in their search.

This experience made them rethink their basic objectives as a community, the community's vocation. They realized that the laity they were to serve were also a source of energy for them. Co-operation with the laity became a significant objective for the community. They made a commitment to a process for bringing it about, reflecting their new sense of mission as communal.

They realized that acknowledging achievements, failures, joys and sorrows as well as communal celebration must include the laity in the future.

A criterion of future discernment: Later, when significant ministerial decisions had to be made, the community returned to their experience of consolation. Thus when it was a question of opening a new ministry among the poor in a hostile climate they recalled this experience of communal spiritual consolation.

When they went through the steps for making such decisions they included this experience as a new element in their decision-making process. It became a part of their 'God story' as a community. It was an event they remembered in their communal graced history.

For judging their state of being as they made ministerial decisions, they recalled this communal spiritual consolation and asked themselves whether the present situation involved all or some of the experiences of that event.

This example answers many of the questions spiritual masters point to when testing the spirits in individual persons (cf. 1 Jn 4:1–18). What is the source of the experience? How does it develop and grow? What is the end result of the experience?

When we consider this communal experience, what can we recognize that parallels our understanding of individual discernment of spirits? What would we sense carries us beyond individual to communal discernment?

We notice that there was a movement from disbelief and aloneness to one of interpersonal unity, trust and hope; from communal desolation to communal consolation.

The movement itself was unexpected, a surprise. The community experienced an increase of faith, hope, love and peace in the midst of great sorrow and loss.

We also recognize in the experience of this community some of the faith experiences we tend to think only apply to individual persons. They have experienced the One, the Beautiful, the True, the Good, even though it was not in the dramatic way that the chosen people experienced the God of Abraham, Isaac and Jacob with Moses on Mount Sinai (cf. Ex 19:16–26).

They were given an experience of being loved *as a community*. This led to a new sense of belonging and togetherness and then a new sense of unity and communal identity. Moreover, the origin of this consolation came from outside the community, i.e., from the larger faith community through whose actions the love of God was experienced.

The community experienced new meaning as it realized its identity with the suffering Christ in this experience. In a new-found sense of humility the community was able to take on the mind and heart of Christ somewhat as Paul urged the community of Philippi to do (Ph 2:5–11).

The most complete communal experience, that of liturgy, brought the community to realize it was re-expressing the paschal mystery of Christ. We might say that they had a new consciousness of the risen Christ in their midst. This sense of Christ led to a further desire, resolve and energy for ministry.

We can recognize in this very historical experience the compassion, love, kindness, teaching and strength of God. For this community there is a new conviction that their own and the larger faith community are an expression of the risen Christ. They have been given a new knowledge of how to look for Christ in interpersonal human events. This heightened awareness of Christ in the community has led them to pray that they will search out his presence in ordinary interpersonal life and be instruments of insight, strength, joy and peace in this world.

The memory of this experience will have a special place in the ongoing discernment of this community. It will produce insight and energy each time it is recalled. It will give a sense of belonging to the larger faith community's *memoria* of the Eucharist.

EXERCISE IV: DESCRIBING COMMUNAL CONSOLATION[4]

It seems important for a group to use its memory to get in touch with an experience it would consider a communal spiritual consolation and then attempt to describe it. The following exercise might help the group do this.

The exercise has four parts: private reflection, sharing the results in the group, further reflection on what was shared, and a group awareness of the basic elements of the group's communal spiritual consolation.

Theme: Knowing and describing our communal spiritual consolation

PRIVATE REFLECTION

Context

We always thank God for you all, mentioning you in our prayers continually. We remember before our God and Father how active is the faith, how unsparing the love, how persevering the hope which you have from our Lord Jesus Christ. (1 Th 1:2, 3)

Imaging

I imagine myself at various events of our communal history where I consider we as a community have experienced the consolations of God (togetherness, unity, beauty, truth, goodness, peace, joy, sorrow, faith, hope, love).

... the fruit of the Spirit is love, joy, peace, patience, kindness, goodness, trustfulness, gentleness and self-control. (Ga 5:22)

The grace desired

I ask the Lord to enlighten my mind and move my heart so that I will get in touch with our communal consolation and be able to describe it.

Points

Occasion: I begin by recalling evident moments of the felt presence of God in our history: events, persons, world situations.
- When and where in our history did this consolation occur?
- What were we about?

Description: Then I reflect on these moments and these gifts to get in touch with them to be able to describe them. It may help to describe our communal consolation by comparing the experiences with some of my personal experiences of spiritual consolation. I would describe my experience of our communal consolation under these headings:

Dying/Rising

Images/Feelings

Insights/Concepts

GROUP SHARING

Each person in the group shares the event chosen and the description.

REFLECTION ON THE GROUP'S SHARING

Each person reflects for a few minutes to discover the common elements expressed by the group.

FURTHER AWARENESS

The group shares the common elements discovered, and discusses what it will look for when questioning whether the group is in spiritual consolation.

NOTES

[1] St Augustine also speaks of movement when he describes charity: 'By charity I mean the movement of the soul towards the enjoyment of God for his own sake' (*De Doctrina Christi* iii, 10).

[2] Michael Buckley sj has developed this insight extensively in his article 'The Structure of the Rules for Discernment of Spirits', in *The Way Supplement* 20 (Autumn 1973), pp. 19–37. Brian O'Leary and I discussed this article, concluding that there is always an element of uplift in consolation that carries one forward even if it is not exactly pleasant, for example, an experience of sweet sorrow.

[3] This example, with some changes, was the basis of my article 'Communal Spiritual Consolation', in the *Review for Religious* (Vol. 47, #6, 1988), pp. 849–57.

[4] Cf. *ISECP* manual, volume 1, pp. 129–130.

4

ESTABLISHING CHRISTIAN COMMUNITY: THE STORY COMPONENT

The history of Christianity is decisive in determining the central meaning of the concept of memory. Christianity has penetrated the space of the Greek logos and its metaphysics as a community of memory and narrative. It is aware that its memories are related to a single historical event in which humanity has been irrevocably redeemed and set free in the eschatological sense by God. From the formal point of view, memory has been taken into the context of faith and freedom. At this time, it has also ceased to be a purely archaeological repetition backwards, as Kierkegaard described Plato's anamnesis. In Christianity, memory is, in its eschatological orientation, a repetitive memory forwards.

(Johannes B. Metz)[1]

We have seen that the secret of discernment is to make decisions in the time of communal spiritual consolation, that is, when there is the experience of God's love present in the group. We need to cultivate a sensitivity to that presence by reflecting on our spiritual experiences, sharing them with others, discerning their meanings in a communal setting and, finally, making any decision to act in response to the call of God we have discerned. The instrument for articulating experience and reflecting upon it is story. Sharing story – the story of each member's personal life and the group's communal journey with God – is both a means of creating community and also an instrument for ongoing communal discernment.

Sharing our stories is not easy. People fear self-revelation because it leaves them vulnerable to ridicule. We have to work against our culture which does not encourage us to give each other the gift of patient listening. It may be hard for people to believe not only that their story is important but that anyone else cares to know it. Some people simply have never developed the skills needed to express

59

themselves. Some may be inhibited because they feel unsure of being able to see the significance of their experience.

Nevertheless, sharing our story is how we discover and communicate God's presence in our day-to-day experience. As a group comes to understand that its life experiences, its personal and communal histories, are a revelation from God to be reflected upon and prayed over, then it will be able to give itself more fully to the activity of sharing story.

The sharing of our 'graced histories' involves speaking and listening. How one speaks out one's own history and listens to the other person's history is important in creating community. A story has to be heard or it is not a story. Persons need to acquire the skills of telling their stories and listening to the stories of the other members of the community.

What is the story?

For years the Israelites shared their story of the Exodus from slavery in Egypt, as Jews continue to do to the present day.

> 'In times to come, when your child asks you, "What is the meaning of the instructions, laws and customs which Yahweh our God has laid down for you?" you are to tell your child, "Once we were Pharaoh's slaves in Egypt, and Yahweh brought us out of Egypt by a mighty hand. Before our eyes, Yahweh worked great and terrible signs and wonders ·against Egypt, against Pharaoh and his entire household. And Yahweh brought us out of there, to lead us into the country which Yahweh had sworn to our ancestors to give us. And Yahweh has commanded us to observe all these laws and to fear Yahweh our God, so as to be happy for ever and to survive, as we do to this day." '
>
> (Dt 6:20–4)

Each year the eldest in the family tells the story of the great deeds of God in releasing the Israelites from the oppression of Pharaoh. These stories found their place in the Bible, and are still at the heart of the Jewish sense of identity as the people of God.

Christian community first occurred, it might be said, as the disciples recounted their experience of meeting the risen Jesus. 'Then they told their story of what had happened on the road and how they had recognized him at the breaking of bread' (Lk 24:35). As the young community persevered in 'the breaking of bread and the prayers', at the heart of their thanksgiving (Eucharist) was the story of Jesus taking bread on the night that he was betrayed. This strong memory (Greek *anamnesis*, Latin *memoria*) was (as with the Israelites before them) the making of community. The act of remembering, re-telling the story, is a much more dynamic experience in both Jewish and Christian life than the rather shallow notion of memory, as popularly understood, might suggest. The Hebrew Testament witnesses to the creative power of the word in Israel's religion. Christians not only keep alive the past by re-telling the story of the paschal mystery, the passover of Jesus, but they are themselves enlivened as they make the passover with him, as the body of which he is the head.

Telling the story

Each Christian's story is told, and heard, in the light of this story, each Christian community is formed and grows as it discovers its identity in the body of Christ by the hearing and telling of its individual and communal stories. Telling one's story is the initial instrument for the members of a community to begin truly to listen to each other and to gain a heightened awareness of the Spirit's activity among them. The person telling is risking self; the persons listening are opened up and discover and risk themselves. Sharing becomes an instrument of affirmation and trust, and so gives the group a new awareness of being community. The consoling sense of God's presence in this activity becomes the basis for the group's further discernment of its state and of its future action. And when such discernment is practised as a way of life, 'telling the story' takes on its proper importance.

Our life as revelation: a conversion experience

There is a kind of conversion involved here. We are given 'eyes to see and ears to hear' so that we can appreciate the unique way that God relates to us. We realize that both the individual and the communal experiences of the group are being approached in a new way. New ways of understanding our lives and our life together are being opened up. Life is revelation, and our life story and stories become God's word to us as we see them in the perspective of the paschal mystery of Jesus Christ. Jesus as 'Lord of history' takes on a fresh meaning for us.

All history is graced history

Believing that Jesus Christ is the meaning of the events of human living makes all history graced history. God is present to it all. When we are in touch with our light history we recall the joyful, blessed events of our lives. Similarly we can focus on desolate, hope-filled, suffering, challenging or call events, and even on the sinful, dark events in our history. Our sin history, too, is graced for we only know that we are sinners in the context of God's grace. It is the love of God that reveals our sin to us. In this way we discover riches we did not know and we realize deeper experiences of affective relationship with God. Our experience is where God has been with us and so it becomes matter for our prayer whether it brings sorrow or joy.

Recognizing our myth

The searching out and expressing of the meaning found in the events brings persons into the mystery, or myth, of their lives. Myth, in the sense that it explains things, helps people to understand who they are and what their purpose is. Myth is not fiction but an imaginative explanation that carries with it a truth that is larger than individual events. As the years pass by new experiences colour

our old experiences and further meaning is given. Recognizing the presence of its myth is part of the communal spiritual consolation that a community is seeking as it reflects and plans and seeks confirmation for its decisions. When the Second Vatican Council urged religious communities of women and men to return to the spirit of their founders, members were encouraged to tell the history of their community so as to get in touch with its basic myth, vision, dreams, hopes and desires.

A new identity

This stage is reached when after some time of being together and after their sharing of individual stories with their hopes and desires, visions and images, sense of call and other interior experiences, the group can begin to recognize and share its own communal history. There is a union of vision, dreams, hopes and desires which gives rise to a felt communal identity. The group as a whole comes to know itself as a community, limited and sinful, but gifted too with a call beyond itself for the betterment of humanity. Fundamentally, it can know it is 'the beloved of God'.

The persons in the community now have a new perspective and horizon. They begin to realize that their communal life is the place of God, and their word of God for prayer. They take on a spirituality of community. They desire to see the community grow in love within itself and beyond itself. They acknowledge the disorder and sinfulness of the community. They image the community (in the context of the whole church) as the body of Christ. The eyes and ears of each person praying in the community now focus on the giftedness of all the members of the community. They recognize experientially, 'There are many different gifts, but it is always the same Spirit' (1 Co 12:4). They realize affectively, 'We, although there are many of us, are one single body' in Christ (1 Co 10:17). Out of this they know that in some way they will relive communally the life, suffering, death and resurrection of Christ.

DEVELOPMENTS IN SHARING OUR STORIES

Experience, the starting point

We begin by remembering our experience. This reflects a great shift in spirituality and decision-making in the last forty to fifty years; experience has become the starting point. Our experience is important, it is to be trusted, it is to be the basis of decision.

In the activity of recalling, appreciating and appropriating our graced history we are recognizing God's presence in our past experiences, however incomprehensible they are. We also heighten our awareness of God's unique presence with us now. Past experiences can be brought into our present decision-making situation. They can be used to judge whether we are experiencing true spiritual consolation as we make decisions.

Memory, anamnesis

The memory evoked in these activities is similar to the one that a community of Christians recalls when celebrating the Eucharist. The faith community's special memory is the activity by which people identify with the experience of Jesus, the Apostles, Paul and the historical church. When people appreciate themselves as part of this experience, they are experiencing tradition.

As one shares one's life experience with others and searches with them to know its meaning in terms of the paschal mystery of Jesus, one is using this kind of memory to appreciate and appropriate one's life history. Such dynamic memory enables the person to find meaning and to be present to life history as graced history.

As people share their stories in a faith community two memories are operative: the memory of the individual recalling experiences of life from a faith perspective and the memory of the faith community that is listening. Both of these memories are significant for the teller and the listeners. The faith memory of the community becomes a criterion for discerning the experience that is being shared. When the community senses a harmony between the story being told and its own faith memory it will be able to affirm the experience as one from the Lord. This interplay helps the individual and the community to know and describe this spiritual consolation.

A contemplative experience

If we approach sharing as an opportunity to be with Christ and those who belong to his body then it can become a contemplative experience. We start to approach each other differently and we are open to structuring our meetings to assist us to be what we are, an expression of the body of Christ. When we share our story we open ourselves to the whole community's story and start to establish the bonding that helps us to approach the meeting as a contemplative experience.[2] Then the other activities of the gathering, no matter how challenging and critical, will be appreciated as part of this contemplation.

Eventually we discover that this sharing is a new form of prayer and a new experience of the presence of God to us. We realize that we are all limited, sinful, yet beloved of God. We begin to recognize our own giftedness and the giftedness of the other members and we gradually have an experience of church. We become a community of faith. So we move from a life of isolation and individualism to one of community and we are given a new realization of the presence of Christ not only in the word of scripture and the Eucharist but also in this small faith-sharing Christian community.

Learning to listen

Listening to the experiences of others and the works of the Spirit in them gives us a sense of awe and gratitude toward God and a respect and trust of the other members of the group. It helps us recognize our unity in spite of our diversity. A group may find it helpful to go through some exercises to develop its listening skills. Listening goes beyond hearing. All the senses are working although hearing is primary. One's whole person is involved in listening.

What is being shared is personal experiences. This means the one speaking is the expert. The role of the listener then is to listen attentively with a non-critical attitude. We are not to make judgements about the moral worth of the person speaking nor the activities they are relating. It is important to listen carefully to the story itself. Since the person speaking is talking basically about experiences of God in his or her life, the listener is relating to the words as an expression of the Spirit no matter who is speaking. The listener can then recognize where there is a harmony with his or her own experience of God. Listening requires humility and self-forgetfulness. The listener takes on an attitude of appreciation of the gift being presented by the speaker, reaching out to hear what is being said. Listening is a sacrifice of self.

Learning to tell our story

How do we tell our story? Much the same way that the disciples on the way to Emmaus did. They related their experiences of desolation, 'Our own hope had been . . .', and consolation, 'Did not our hearts burn within us as he . . . explained the scriptures to us?' (Lk 24: 13–32)

A certain consciousness of time is helpful in telling our story. Yet it is important that we feel free to take as much time as we need. We can rely on the willingness of others to listen to us with open hearts. Eventually, we learn how to speak briefly yet with enough concreteness that others will be able to relate to our experience and gain insights into their own.

Gradually people learn how to share certain intimate experiences that are important to them in their relationship with God. These intimate experiences may have been with loved ones and/or with the persons of the Trinity. Initially all they may be able to tell are external events of their story. This is enough at the beginning until they have gained trust in the group or have learned how to understand and express intimate experiences.

Feedback

An important activity in the sharing of story is feedback. After a first go-round of sharing, the members may remain quietly reflecting on what impressed them as they listened. Then a further brief sharing can let the others know they have been heard and appreciated. This is the cement that binds the group together. Eventually the experience of the group gets highlighted. The community is concerned about the concrete, historical events affecting it.

The experience of communal spiritual consolation

As a group shares its personal and communal histories certain changes take place. The group starts to express a new understanding and awareness of the reasons for its existence and of how it is to live. It now shares a new sense of identity as a community and a new sense of the spiritual. The members will usually indicate a further level of commitment with each other in terms of time, sharing and action.

They begin to acknowledge the significance and impact of the group on their very persons and not just on the activities and time commitments. Eventually they communicate their appreciation of this community and the awareness that it is a gift from the Lord. They point out to each other the awareness of Christ in their midst as they appreciate Jesus' statement: 'For where two or three meet in my name, I am there among them' (Mt 18:20). Then they hear from each other words such as, 'I am part of this group.' 'This is my community, after all.' 'We'-statements instead of 'I'-statements: 'We may be small, limited and even sinful. Still, we are called together in the Lord to help to build up a world of peace, justice and love.'

The ability grows to 'say it as it is' in situations of tension and crisis arising from personality differences in the group. The group may go into mutual self-revelation and keep communicating until an acceptance of each other and a new sense of bonding take place. The group expresses in humility that it is limited, sinful and disordered. Then they may express their desire to work for a society

67

of justice, love, joy and peace, even while acknowledging and accepting their limitations (creaturehood) and disordered tendencies (sinfulness). Now they willingly state their commitment to discern with the community the concrete expression of their call.

Eventually their expressions change from 'I am the beloved of God' to 'We are the beloved of God'. They recognize and express a sense of communal freedom and communal desire. Now they are able to state their sense of the mystery they experience in the group and their awareness that God is experienced among them.

EXERCISE V: PRAYING OVER THE COMMUNITY'S HISTORY

The following communal prayer exercise may help a group become a community or help a community develop more fully. (Some readers will recognize that these exercises are similar to those found in the manual *Ignatian Spiritual Exercises for the Corporate Person*. I am indebted to the other authors of this manual for permission to use it.)

A chief way of helping a group to affirm its identity is to share various common experiences of the past. If the group has been in existence for some time or has some common roots of national or religious identity the prayer and sharing over its communal history is a good instrument for affirming its identity. Such prayer is best done through a number of sessions that include the group's 'light history', 'dark history', 'call history', 'suffering history', and 'joy-filled history'.

There are five steps in these exercises: a communal gathering of prayer material; prayerful reflection with the material gathered; sharing the results of this prayer; reflecting on the sharing, and a brief further sharing. The group may wish to refer to the two notes on the exercise at the end of Chapter 2 (page 44).

Theme: Prayer on our communal graced light history

COMMUNAL PREPARATION

Contextualizing

With so many witnesses in a great cloud all around us, we too, then, should throw off everything that weighs us down . . . and with perseverance keep running in the race which lies ahead of us. Let us keep our eyes fixed on Jesus, who leads us in our faith and brings it to perfection. (Heb 12:1, 2)

Imaging

I imagine myself with all the members of our group as they go about with the Lord developing the reign of God. I pay special attention to the blessed moments of our story.

The grace desired

We seek from the Holy Spirit (Jn 14:26) a sense of appreciation of how God has been gracious and faithful to us that we may more generously respond to God's continual revelation to us.

Pointing (in the group)

Reflect quietly for about ten minutes on the following and jot down the points that come to your mind. Then share with one another and jot down further points that impress you.

- Recall the significant persons of our history.
  Recall the cultural setting of this history.
  Recall the mission, expansion and the achievements of our history.

- Reflect on the membership, the spiritual experiences and the life-style of our history.
  Reflect on the way in which this spirit was present and showed itself as our history developed.

- What impresses me about our history?

PRIVATE REFLECTION

I pray with the material generated in the Pointing.

I consider our history in terms of the many blessings we have received through these years.

I remember different persons, places, situations and the historical state of the world at the different times of our group's history.

After this time of remembering I ponder the continual presence of God with us during these years.

COMMUNAL SHARING

Private review of prayer

- I spend some time reflecting on what happened to me in this time of prayer, for example, significant moments; insights; different affections; experiences of consolation and desolation.
- What experiences of these years are significantly present to me now?
- What does this arouse in me?

Then the group shares the fruits of their prayer.

FURTHER REFLECTION ON OUR GROUP SHARING

- What did I hear?
- What impressed me as the others shared?
- What new insights did I gain?
- What are the inevitable consequences of the truths we have shared?
- Where did I experience affective harmony with the others as they spoke about our history?

FURTHER SHARING FROM THE PREVIOUS REFLECTION

We speak briefly to each other saying what moved us as the others shared the results of their prayer.

We speak to God in appreciation and anticipation:
- an expression of wonder at the ways God has drawn our community together.
- an expression of gratitude that God has been with the persons and events of our history up until now.
- an expression of openness to the directions we perceive in our history.

NOTES

[1] *Faith in History and Society: Towards a Practical Fundamental Theology* (Crossroads, New York, 1979), p. 188.
[2] Cf. note 2, chapter 5, p. 88.

THE CHALLENGE OF EXPRESSING OUR STORY

If we live by the truth and in love, we shall grow completely into Christ, who is the head by whom the whole Body is fitted and joined together, every joint adding its own strength, for each individual part to work according to its function. So the body grows until it has built itself up in love.

(Ep 4:15–16)

I recall a community of six men and three women who were facing the possibility of changing their total life-style and place of residence or disbanding and going their separate ways. In this crisis they felt called to risk themselves in sharing as never before. They had to search their inner beings for more self-knowledge and their commitment to be a community. But mostly they had to find the courage to be open and honest with each other.

As the group reviewed its history it was obvious that different viewpoints were being expressed. Then one of the women spoke to one of the men: 'You really hurt me when you made that decision in the back room with your two male colleagues. All of us need to be informed and present when communal decisions are made.' This in turn raised the hackles of the male. Further interchange about secrecy and a clique mentality took place. Eventually what surfaced was the sense that the group was controlled not by itself but by another authoritative body within it. The group's leader was the spokesperson for the smaller in-group.

Then the whole group reviewed its history and expressed in an open way how it had been wounded by the controlling group. Members confronted the leader and insisted that proper discernment procedures take place. Interestingly, the leader had actually been wanting to develop proper discerning procedures. Only with the need for a serious decision to continue in a new way or to disband had the moment of openness, risk and freedom arrived.

It is not always easy to share. Intimacy can be hard-won. So let's take a closer look at what we mean by the sharing of the story in community. We have seen that it is essential for developing community and we know that it is an important part of making communal decisions. What we want to explore now is the question of 'How?', for the way personal or group story is expressed influences the group's experience of spiritual consolation because it is in the sharing of story that the group becomes aware of movements of spirit both in individuals and the group as a whole.

A community may encounter many difficulties with public expression. Some members may be unwilling to share. Others may have trouble finding the correct words to share. The introverts in a group may feel oppressed by the extroverts' apparent ease of expression. A third challenge may be recognizing the level of sharing; members may be challenged to encourage deeper levels of sharing. Of great importance is discerning the communal significance of what is shared.

Experience, intentionality and expression

Everyone hungers to be heard and understood. Being with others who also share the story of their life journeys helps one find a support community of people of like minds. Expressing oneself in this way enhances self-understanding and listening to others leads to growth in appreciation of them.

As a group acknowledges its history as a group it begins to discover its identity. Over time it will experience a natural movement that will be expressed by the members wondering 'What is our purpose? What more will we do?' A support group like a twelve-step group (e.g., Alcoholics Anonymous and others similar) may decide that they simply want to continue to come together and share. (I would argue that this is a group rather than a community because it is not committed as a body to ongoing relationship with the persons nor to a concerted effort outside itself other than possibly extending its message of support to potential new members.) Because of the way they listen and support each other the members of such a group may experience the unconditional love of the group, and that may be sufficient. But I am not talking about a gathering where people may experience love and acceptance and be inspired to help others individually and continue to come together in an association which they support by individual decisions. Rather, I am talking about a small group that starts to get a sense of itself as a corporate being – something that may not happen until it has been meeting for several years – and then moves to a questioning of its purpose as an *entity*. Someone may become the voice of the group and say something like, 'I think I want deeper commitment. This faith-sharing is wonderful, but can we share more of our lives? Does anyone else feel this way?' If trust has been established through sharing story, people can feel free to respond to this expression of one person's desire for the group. The group can begin to explore itself as a corporate being.

As the possibility of greater commitment to each other surfaces among members and the group starts to grapple with it, various movements come to the surface: members experience hope, fears, desires, enthusiasm, discouragement, and positive and negative images of commitment and authority. Questions like 'Who's in charge?' emerge. People need to reflect patiently together on all these interior experiences, to look at what is happening inside themselves and to express it.

The stirrings increase if the group looks at the possibility of action that will carry it beyond itself, because this invites members to consider a whole new set of commitments. The group needs to determine where these reactions are coming from in order to become clear on what is motivating them with respect to the proposed action. The underlying motivations may be altruistic, or they may be selfish. As members discuss their thoughts, feelings, hopes, dreams and fears, they may find that they are being motivated by guilt, peer pressure, or a desire for recognition. Are they moving out of concern for others? Are they responding to a call from the poor? Are they thinking about going into action so that they will not have to share more deeply with each other? They may have to decide whether they are being manipulated by a fanatic in the group or moved by a true prophet. Considering the answers to such questions is the beginning of the process of the discernment of spirits.

The basic question for the group, as for an individual engaged in discernment, is how to discover whether it is being motivated by the love of God. Thus the basic process is one of sensitively looking at their experiences, particularly the affective dimension, in order to discover the overall direction of the movement, its intending. Where is the group being drawn? What is pulling or pushing it? Are members being motivated by love? Because love is the central issue, they must pay particular attention to their affective experiences and examine motivations at the deepest feeling level. To discover whether a desire is motivated by love, it must be examined over time; reflection on its source or beginning, how it is now, and its probable ultimate outcome will help to reveal this. A call that is from God will move the group into action that manifests unconditional love. Only people who want to be lovers discern. The issue always is whether we are being true or false lovers.

To make these judgements one uses as points of reference one's experiences of being loved by God. Individuals in the group will probably have had particular experiences of being drawn by God's love flooding their hearts through their interaction with other people, possibly with other group members. Such experiences may have occurred when they were with the larger faith community at the Eucharist. Exploring the qualities of this experience gives people a heightened awareness of their affective relationship with God for the time of reflection on and discernment of a communal decision.

Shared reflection on the intentionality within personal and communal experience is in itself an experience. Sharing insights about the possible direction in which we are being drawn heightens awareness of the personal and communal experiences under consideration. This creates a cycle: expression brings about a new experience because the heightening of awareness is in itself an experience with its own intentionality that will emerge as it is expressed and reflected on by the community. This can be compared to the experience individuals may have when they use gestures in prayer to deepen interior experiences in a group setting, heightening a group's experience of the affective movements of its relationship with God.

Sometimes the intentionality or sense of being drawn toward God and out of self, individual or communal, is immediately clear right in the experience itself. There is a juxtaposition of interpersonal presence and intention in experiences of being loved, being called forth, or surrendering to God's love. The intentionality within such an experience may occur through an ecstatic utterance, a prophecy, or another religious experience of an individual's being carried beyond him- or herself. Or such an experience may unite a special sense of one's identity with a particular decision and action. This was the case with the disciples of whom we read, 'And at once they left their nets and followed him' (Mk 1:18).

More often, especially in group situations, the intentionality is hidden and the experiences need to be described and interpreted so that the full significance of hopes, dreams, desires, contemplation and images can be known.

How people express themselves

For a discerning process to take place people have to move to different levels of revelation and understanding. Reflection deepens as individuals get feedback from the group, in a continuous process. Ways of expression differ; some people do not express their deepest experiences of God in words or even gestures but through their lives in action for others. Expressing one's interior attitudes and inner state of being is most often through words but body language may well be part of a community's interaction. The way the group gathers and worships as well as the way it shares and how it makes decisions are all aspects of its communication. And hidden within every bit of it is the intentionality that moves and energizes the group.

The depth of the community's self-knowledge as well as the depth of members' commitment to each other depends on external expression. It is through this that it comes to recognize itself as a corporate entity and corporate person or subject. Even in the silence and stillness of a Quaker meeting there is an external expression: they have gathered together. The meeting is an expression of dependence on the Spirit for speech and an expression of fellowship in silence. The silence itself is a symbol of awe and presence before

God. It also prepares the way for reverential listening to those who are moved to speak.

As a group grows into a faith community the sharing becomes more and more trusting and eventually deeper. As the group moves from simple sharing of events to add hopes, desires, vision, dreams and images of reality, spiritual vocabulary increases and ways of communication change. In the sharing, the members of the community eventually express the way they image themselves in relation to God, where they find God and how they live out their spiritual lives. Members notice the recurrence of expressions that indicate a faith community is present. Some of these have to do with where the community senses God; some with the sense of mystery; some with a new understanding and appreciation of history; some with the felt sense of the risen Lord in the community. The community learns to describe its interior movements. It begins to recognize communal experiences that energize and move the community as a whole.

EXPRESSION AND DISCERNMENT

1. What is being expressed

As we have seen in chapter 4, for Christians to share their stories is the way they discover and communicate God's presence in their day to day experience. To do this well requires a number of activities which constantly interact with each other: reflection on experience for a heightened awareness of the presence of God in their life experiences, the choosing of words to express this awareness, and a sensitivity to those listening. In the reflection on experience people try to get in touch with the hidden elements. They try to discover the images underpinning their interior experiences.

Initially, persons may only be able to express external events to the other members of the group. Then they learn to express their feelings about experiences they have had. Then they are able to talk about the felt presence or absence of God. Eventually, they can express in more refined language the intimacy of the experience with God.

The development of this ability to express one's interior state in spiritual terminology usually means that the persons in the group gradually learn a new language using words and phrases such as spiritual consolation, spiritual desolation, dryness in prayer, temptation, inner peace, joy, suffering with Christ and call.

2. Description of this spirituality

(A) LOCALE OF THE DIVINE

As members of the group tell their story, their images of God and of themselves in relation to God begin to emerge: the perspective, that is, in which they live their personal lives.

In a developed faith community members believe that the Deuteronomic expression, 'The word is very near to you, it is in your mouth and in your heart for you to put into practice' (Dt 30:14 and Rm 10:8), refers to the community's mouth and heart. The mystery of God and neighbour will be recognized in communal activity. The presence of God is found in living and working through communal processes and decision-making. Sacraments are now appreciated as expressions of personal relationship and more than things or actions to be done; they are the interchange and commitments persons have with each other.

As they share, their belief that Jesus reveals the divine in the human gets expressed. In this belief the full impact of Jesus' earthly life is operative. His earthly life gives them an awareness of the mystery of the human as well as the divine. They express the mystery of their believing community in terms of the presence of the risen Christ. Again, the belief is expressed that they can move beyond a knowing about the divine through studying the teachings of Christ, to an experiencing of the divine. They believe experiencing the divine is similar to the way the disciples knew Jesus. This experiencing of the divine is knowing the risen Christ in the very faith community to which they belong. It is an immediate experience of 'the church, which is his body, the fullness of him who is

78

filled, all in all' (Ep 1:22, 23). Each person comes to realize that other humans are not distractions to higher prayer and union with God, but the medium of the presence of the divine. They believe and recognize the scripture statements, 'God created humankind in the image of God' (Gn 1:27); 'We are God's work of art, created in Christ Jesus for . . . good works' (Ep 2:10).

(B) AN HISTORICAL PERSPECTIVE

The historical quality of this spirituality is expressed in recounting personal and communal graced history. As each person's graced history is unique so each community will have its unique communal spirituality because each community has the experience of its own communal graced history.

Spirituality is discovered in the operative images of God, the world, the church, community and myself that I have and express. The desires that flow from these images also indicate my spirituality. These images and desires flow from our experiences of life in Christian community. From one's baptism forward a person who has grown up in a Christian atmosphere is influenced by Christian community. The ways this person has imbibed life and faces life decisions will have a Christian-community aspect to it. This applies to the Christian community experienced in childhood and adolescence as Lutheran, Anglican, Evangelical, Methodist, Orthodox, Roman Catholic or whatever Christian community. It is important to acknowledge and get in touch with these historical and often hidden influences of Christian community in one's spiritual life.

3. What expressions indicate that an authentic spirituality of community is being enfleshed?

Once a group is committed to a spirituality of community, its heightened awareness gets expressed in its desires, ideals, symbols and images, prayer, discernment and conversion experiences. This awareness of a spirituality of community changes the motivating energy of a group. It changes attitudes and judgements both within

79

the community and beyond. The desires of the group change. Conversions are experienced and judged differently.

The expressions in a Christian community indicate that to belong to it is more than friendship in a club or the sense of team spirit in a sport or a business venture. It is different from the wedding covenant between two persons and their families. Ideally, there is openness to all other human beings. The members look for covenanted relationships beyond that of the spouse and the family. These are acknowledged as something given by the Holy Spirit, as experienced in the interior of one's being as well as in the external relationships among the members of the community. It brings the members to a sense of identity with each other in the Lord. We might say it is an experience of the risen Christ in the midst of the community. It leads people to new levels of interpersonal intimacy, to new desires and ways of building the realm of justice, peace, love and joy among all humans. In all this there is a new experiential perspective or horizon from which life is understood. This results in changed attitudes and practices of prayer, worship, life decisions and actions. Through the gift of the Holy Spirit corporate union, love, suffering, disagreements, conflicts, joy and peace are experienced anew.

As the group grows into a Christian community it becomes aware of a sense of mystery operating in itself. This sense of mystery becomes an aspect of its spirituality of community and an object of its hope and expectation as well as a point of reference when it discerns its well-being and instrumentality with Christ in the world.

The ellipse with its two foci might be a good visual symbol, with one focal point being each individual's experience and the other being the other members' experiences. It is their interchanges that bring about community, and community is more than the horizontal relationship or dialogue between the two foci. Total experience as represented by the ellipse includes the larger dimension or mystery that is an experience of the body of the risen Christ. The community embraces all the individuals but in such a way that their freedom is enhanced.

Christian community is akin to the experience of family and clan in that there is a life-line connectedness among all the members. There is an acknowledgement of bonding with the other members. This bonding will mean different things in different expressions of

Christian community. Also, as we have seen, because the group is Christian it cannot be chauvinistic; as an expression of Christ, the bondedness and intimacy will not turn in on itself but open itself to the people of God, the human race.

Christian community is also an experience of Christian fellowship. Fellowship involves a covenant relationship of Christ with the church and the human race. Christian community is built on spiritual bondedness and intimacy regardless of blood lines. Through various processes of investigation, dialogue and sharing, members of a Christian community grow in their commitment to each other.

Such companionship in the Lord is well described in scripture. The early church gives us a clear expression of this companionship. The sharing of everything – property, food, prayer, miraculous powers and the good news of Jesus Christ – was the sign of their communion with each other in the Lord.

Recognition of movement of the Holy Spirit in the early church always carried the community beyond itself; they were able to recognize the activity of God beyond their own experience of fellowship. This is most noteworthy in the experience of Peter with Cornelius in Acts 10. Peter went in violation of the Jewish customs to visit the pagan Cornelius. He spoke to Cornelius and his family about Jesus Christ. 'While Peter was still speaking the Holy Spirit came down on all the listeners . . . Peter himself then said, "Could anyone refuse the water of baptism to these people, now they have received the Holy Spirit just as we have?" ' (Ac 10:44–7).

Impact on life-style

The basic impact of this spirituality on the group's life-style is heightened appreciation of the communal experiences of life. The group comes to reflect on its life in terms of the life of Christ. This means that it uses the life-death-resurrection experience of Christ as a paradigm for understanding its own life experiences. The group realizes that it may re-experience some of the life of the early church with its joys, sufferings, sins and virtues. In the intimacy of a committed communal life they look to experience the risen Christ in their midst. So they may recognize the experience of the growing wisdom of Christ, the courage of Christ, the compassion of Christ, the healing power of Christ, the committed suffering of Christ and the joys of Christ.

Faith communities come to see themselves, in humility, as instruments and expressions of Christ in our world. They see that their very effort to become a Christian faith community is already a sign of the risen Christ to themselves and to the world. They also recognize that a true expression of Christian community demands that they have an outward concern for those beyond their immediate community. In the true understanding of hope, they know this concern is to go out to the whole world.

As community grows, members listen to and reflect on the scriptures and prayers of the Eucharist differently. They become very conscious of the communal aspect of scripture and the Eucharist. Their images of themselves before God are communal. This overflows in their desires and prayers to God.

They have a new sense of Eucharist: Christ is not in our midst, but is our midst.[1] This Christ is a new context for understanding. 'And as there is one loaf, so we, although there are many of us, are one single body, for we all share in the one loaf' (1 Co 10:17).

When it comes to making communal decisions they attempt as a community to read the signs of the times. They remember their communal graced history as a criterion for making decisions. So they are able to recognize the gifts of the Spirit in the community (Ga 5:22, 23); the living out of Paul's appeal to the Philippians to live a life of oneness in thought, love and action (Ph 2:1–5); the Beatitudes (Mt 5:1–12); the great criterion of Christ: 'In so far as you did this to one of these least ones you did it to me' (Mt 25:40). They are able to experience in a new way the expression of Paul and to find the glory on the face of Christ in the human face of our own modern world: 'And all of us, with unveiled faces, seeing the glory of the Lord as though reflected in a mirror, are being transformed into the same image from one degree of glory to another; for this comes from the Lord, the Spirit' (2 Co 3:18, *Good News Bible*). These communities accept Paul's horizon that Christians are the body of Christ and they look for experiences of Christ in the very interchange among themselves. Knowing that everyone suffers in this life, they look for meaningful ways of doing this in Christ in the interchange that takes place in community and as their community looks beyond itself. They see a more immediate and real possibility of fulfilling Paul's desire: '[I want to know Christ] and the power of his resurrection, and partake of his sufferings' (Ph 3:10). They envisage a community that expresses the suffering of the risen Christ. So they wish to be open to the processes that bring about communal spiritual awarenesses of creaturehood, sinfulness, call, decision, suffering and joy in this body trying to live and further the reign of God.

Means of communal expression: focus on myth

A group of religious women gathered to discern where they would set up an apostolate and what their life-style would be. Possible locations included sites in the country, in the suburbs, or in the centre of a city devastated by war. Friends and church authorities were suggesting that they run a middle-class school in the suburbs. They prayed to discover where God would be better served. In their discernment they chose to live in the devastated centre of the city and to assist the women in the area to organize themselves so that they could cope with and eventually change their situation.

The dominant element that helped them to come to this decision was the vision of their founder and the early history of their congregation. They reflected on and appropriated these aspects of their myth. They understood the meaning of their name. They could see the young, uneducated women of their early history living in the slums of the big cities and going about assisting poor women to cope materially and giving these women knowledge of the faith and ability to help themselves. They recalled principles from the early years of their foundation: 'Live among the poor. The poor present the face of Christ to you. The poor will educate you and give you a sense of Christ.'

When they considered living in the devastated centre of the city assisting women in a very simple way these images and these statements gave them joy and consolation. In seeking confirmation of their decision they tried to anticipate the hardships and sufferings this would mean to them. Their name and the vision and dream of the early members of their congregation seemed to call them to go with their decision.

It is important, then, for a group to focus on its myth in order to recognize identity and purpose. Two ways for a group to get in touch with and express its myth are the practice of prayerful sharing over the community's history and the developing of a history line. These instruments allow a group to approach its life experiences from a perspective of God's constant presence to it. Recognizing, appreciating and judging the affective dimension of God's presence to the group over time are essential for communal discernment. A series of prayer exercises over the liberating, oppressive, joyful, suffering and call aspects of its life lets it appreciate all its communal experience as communal graced history.

The development of a communal history line is a good adjunct to prayer over the community's graced history. This is a relatively simple but profound instrument. The exercise at the end of this chapter, 'Creating and reflecting with a communal history line', explains how this is done.

Focus on goals and objectives

A further expression of the group takes place as it focuses on goals and objectives and develops programmes. These activities bring about a deeper sense of communal identity. The movement through to discerned decision and action in accord with the group's myth and goals strengthens commitment to each other as a community. During and especially after such decisions and actions the group must evaluate and consider recommendations for further decisions to be discerned.

A group tends to follow a process of evaluation, recommendation, decision and action as it grows in commitment. Each stage of this process, known as the Energy Cycle, demands expression. The group will be most concerned to devote attention to expressing its spiritual state at the time of discerning the decision. The ways it describes communal spiritual consolation or communal spiritual desolation are especially important before the decision is made and when confirmation is sought for a decision. The group is listening for the kinds of expression listed above as well as the ordinary descriptions of consolation and desolation suggested in Chapter 2 (page 33). But the way the group expresses itself in the evaluation, recommendation and action stages is also indicative of the state of the group and its discernment.[2]

EXERCISE VI: CREATING AND REFLECTING WITH A COMMUNAL HISTORY LINE[3]

This is another exercise to assist a group to pray with its communal history. The community is able to revisit the important events to discover their meanings and their emotional impact. It is a further instrument to help the group appropriate its vision, dream and myth.

A line is drawn horizontally about midway on a large sheet of white paper fastened on a wall which everyone can see so that everyone can contribute to its drawing and everyone can appreciate what is being created in its midst.

There are two steps in this exercise:
   1. composing the history line, and
   2. reflecting with our history line.

Theme: Communal history line

COMPOSING OUR HISTORY LINE

Context

'... Yahweh your God continued to support you, just as one carries a child, all along the road you followed until you arrived here.' (Dt 1:31)

Imaging

I imagine myself with all the persons, events, feelings and meanings present in our history.

The grace desired

We want and desire a sense of appreciation of how the Lord has shown graciousness and faithfulness to us that we may more generously respond to God's continual revelation to us.

Pointing

Privately:
- I identify the historically decisive events.
- I remember the affective component.

As a group:
- We compose our history line.
- We begin with the present and work backwards in time according to everyone's memory.
- We place historically decisive events above the line.
- The emotional impact of these events and the significance of the events for the group's identity and future are identified below the line.

REFLECTING WITH OUR HISTORY LINE

Contemplating our history line

- I spend some time reflecting on how we composed our history line.
  I open myself up to the many ways of the Lord in our history. I allow the significance of our history to move my affections.
- What experiences of these years is significantly present to me today?
- What does this arouse in me?

Group shares the above reflection

Reflection on our group sharing

- What impressed me as the others shared?
- What are the inevitable consequences of the truths we have shared?
- Where did I experience affective harmony with the others as they spoke about our history?
- What new insights did I gain?

Colloquy

We pray aloud in ways such as this:
- We thank you Lord for these moments of your presence to us . . .
- We thank you for . . .
- Give us insight to discern the ways that you call us forth . . .
- We pray for courage and strength to follow these your leads that we discern in our history . . .

Other activities

Other activities may help a group recognize how it began, how it has grown, how it has experienced crisis or loss of members, and how it reactivates itself or dies. These activities can assist a group to foster its life forces, face possible death situations and experience new birth. They are instruments to understand the Life Cycle or life-death-resurrection cycle of the group.[4]

Through these activities a group discovers its myth and develops its communal goals, objectives, and programmes. The community's myth is understood in that part of the life cycle where a group gets in touch with the reasons from within itself and from beyond itself that have brought it together. At this level of sharing the group is attempting to express its heritage, its vision, its dreams, its hopes, its desires, and its charism or gift.

Another instrument for helping a group discern comes from the

Myers-Briggs Type Indicator. MBTI is an instrument for helping persons to discover their preferred way of dealing with the world in terms of psychologist Carl Jung's analysis of personality. The MBTI assists persons to understand some of their own behaviour and that of other people. It is a good instrument in groups because it helps the people to be tolerant and to acknowledge the various contributions of other people who approach life differently. The different gifts in the group can be called to the fore and communal decisions will be more complete.[5] The MBTI is based on Jung's thesis that people use sensation, intuition, thinking and feeling in different ways as they relate to the world. Through a series of questions the MBTI helps people discover their preferred functions. In *Facing Your Type*,[6] Jim Borbely sj and George Schemel sj have shown the way the various functions operate best in a decision-making situation. This involves the activity of focusing on the sensate function (S) first, then the intuitive function (N), followed by the thinking function (T) and finally the feeling function (F). This means the group follows an SNTF movement in working through to a discerned decision. Through this the group should have considered all the pertinent data for a correct discernment. Of course this means that everyone has to find ways of expressing sensate, intuitive, thinking and feeling concerns and those whose dominant functions are sensate, intuitive, thinking and feeling should be satisfied that their concerns have been covered.

NOTES

[1]Cf. Gustave Martelet sj: 'In the eyes of the New Testament it is not the risen Christ who must be seen within the world, but the world itself within the risen Christ' ('Resurrection and Eucharist', *Theology Digest* (St Louis University, St Louis, MO, 1977), p. 210).
[2]Judy Roemer has pointed out the importance of cultivating a contemplative presence in group meetings. She writes that each phase of evaluation, recommendation, decision and action can 'bring the group back into a contemplative stance'. See *The Group Meeting as a Contemplative Experience* (pamphlet published by Typrofile Press, Wernersville, Pennsylvania, 1983), p. 8.

[3]Cf. *ISECP* manual, volume 1, pp. 41–4.

[4]These activities have been developed by an American organization called Management Design Incorporated in an instrument known as the Life Cycle or Grid. The ISECP group are convinced that all human experience can be understood as a life-death-resurrection experience. In their *Ignatian Spiritual Exercises for the Corporate Person* they use this instrument in assisting groups to recognize the activity of God's love in their life and to respond to this love in the discerning process (cf. *ISECP* manual pp. 35–40).

[5]For further information on the MBTI see Isabel Briggs Myers with Peter B. Myers: *Gifts Differing* (Consulting Psychologists Press, Palo Alto, CA, 1980), and David Keirsey and Marilyn Bates: *Please Understand Me: Character and Temperament Types* (Prometheus Nemesis Books, Del Mar, CA, 1978).

[6]Jim Borbely sj and George Schemel sj: *Facing Your Type* (Typrofile, Jesuit Spiritual Center, Wernersville, PA, 1978).

6

COMMUNAL SPIRITUAL FREEDOM

Make your own the mind of Christ Jesus:

Who, being in the form of God,
did not count equality with God
something to be grasped.

But he emptied himself,
taking the form of a slave,
becoming as human beings are;
and being in every way
like a human being,
he was humbler yet,
even to accepting death,
death on a cross.

And for this God raised him high,
and gave him the name
which is above all other names;

so that all beings
in the heavens, on earth
and in the underworld,
should bend the knee at the name of Jesus
and that every tongue should acknowledge
Jesus Christ as Lord,
to the glory of God the Father.

(Ph 2:5–11)

EXPERIENCE OF FREEDOM

Decision-making, new identity and freedom

When a community determines that it will use a discerning process to make decisions in the Lord, it moves beyond an image of itself as a faith-sharing group and begins to experience itself as a vibrant part of the church, bringing gospel values to the world. In such a decision-making situation the community discovers it is called to a new sense of identity and freedom. It decides to respond to God, and to God in the world, with this purpose in mind. It senses that it is being called to go beyond itself for the betterment of humanity and it reaches for freedom to do this greater thing. Discerning decisions for the service of humanity brings forth a new identity, that of disciples of the Lord.

Now the community will begin to struggle with its need to gain freedom in its relationships within itself and beyond itself. It will have to accept limitations and creatureliness within itself and in relationship to the larger world. It will also have to face the disorders and sinfulness of its members and their effects within the community and beyond it. As it considers the implications of a call to serve it has to learn to pray for a willingness to be one with Christ suffering.

The freedom in accepting the limits of creaturehood

The community has to face its limitations and accept its dependency on God. A group may desire to be an instrument of God's grace in our world but not be able to come to a sense of its own total dependence on God's grace let alone the limits of its ability to change unjust social structures. It has to develop a sense of realism concerning its own inner workings and its apostolic endeavour to prevent undue discouragement and to strengthen it to persevere in its efforts at deepening its own communal life and its activities for the human race. As they face their limitations, members can draw inspiration from remembering that they have been created in the

91

image and likeness of God, that they are God's work of art, 'created in Christ Jesus for . . . good works' (Ep 2:10).

Awareness of creaturehood and limitation can be instruments of grace. It can bring the community to seek enlightenment, strength and even love for its enemy. It can bring it to a sense of mystery in the affairs of life. An important prayer that may arise from awareness of limitation is prayer for the grace to be co-operative with others. Communal co-operation is the only way that the world will be saved.

Communities can find some peace in their faith in the God who is always faithful to his promises and constantly gives us the energy to continue to build the realm of justice and love. This faith can give them the necessary patience to wait for new energies, new members or a more suitable time for action.

But communities may reject their responsibility when they experience their limitation and dependency. They can fall into fatalism and passivity that can undermine the realization of their deepest desires. At such a time it is important for a community to image itself as a created free instrument of God in the service of humanity. Exercises such as reflecting on graced history may enable communities to appreciate the gift of their being. The Life Cycle and Energy Cycle can open up awareness of the many possible ways of being instruments of God for the service of humanity.

The very experience of creaturehood and limitation may also become occasions for a community to grow, for it is true that a community has many more talents and gifts and powers than an individual has. In fact the sum total of gifts and powers of the members is not as great as the community's corporate giftedness and power. Only communities can create and establish socially grace-ful structures and move against sinful unjust structures. All this is done in the awareness that we are limited created beings who may have to say: 'We are useless servants: we have done no more than our duty' (Lk 17:10). The important thing is to be with Christ in the enterprise, whatever comes from this.

Freedom with respect to sinful tendencies

Sin and disorder are distinct from creaturehood, dependency and limitations. In fact, not accepting creaturehood, dependency and limitation would be a disorder and may be sinful. A discipleship attitude in a community demands freedom from sin and disorder. This freedom is more than the experience of being forgiven, important as forgiveness is. It builds on the healing experience of forgiveness and draws the community beyond a healing, therapeutic understanding of itself to see itself as a discerning community of gospel service for the betterment of humanity.

For its own sense of identity it is important that a community realize that it is sinful and has sinful tendencies. Hopefully this will make the community humble and also help it to be vigilant with respect to its sinful tendencies. In the communal discerning process humility and vigilance are crucial.

It is difficult and painful to attain this freedom. Yet it is important, for just as a community's creative powers are greater than the sum total of the membership, so the sinful effect of a community is greater than the sum of the sins of the members. Thus a community has good reason to be highly motivated to become free of its sinful tendencies.

Disorders may exist in the ways the members interrelate among themselves. These can be destructive, as St Paul points out: 'If you go snapping at one another and tearing one another to pieces, take care: you will be eaten up by one another' (Ga 5:15).

Sins and disorders in a community may also extend beyond the group. One might be pride of self in a communal sense. A community may become an enclave, a clique that judges others in self-righteousness. It may also put in place forces that destroy other individuals, communities or the environment.

While the first awareness of sinfulness may be shocking and discouraging to a community, eventually the community deals with it or dies. When the community in humility acknowledges its sinfulness and seeks forgiveness within its own membership and beyond, a new sense of identity comes about. Now with a new-found faith in God it can realize like the prodigal child, 'We are the sinful beloved of God.'

93

Moreover, a new energy can also be given as the community realizes that Jesus chose sinful apostles to develop his church and to bring the good news to the world. And so they may experience the call in and through their sinfulness to build the Lord's realm of peace, justice and love.

To gain freedom a community can follow certain spiritual exercises that help it discover its social sinfulness and disorder. It can call upon an outside facilitator or communal spiritual director to aid it. But attaining freedom from sin and disordered tendencies is a difficult task and one that is never totally achieved. It is a good sign when a community desires to recognize its sinfulness and to be continually purified. This freedom is such that the community is not overwhelmed by its sinfulness. In the knowledge and acceptance of its sinfulness and in its desire to make reparation and to overcome its faults it also realizes that the Lord chooses sinners to bring gospel values to humanity.

The freedom to respond to call

With new realism regarding itself as a sinful community continually in need of redemption, the community can open itself up to the world beyond it and wish to be an instrument of God's love for all humanity. It now seeks the freedom to be open to the full vision of the Christian life in order to be a responsible agent of that vision in the world. It is the sense of gratitude that opens up the community to vocation and mission. As disciples in the Lord the community can consider the ways it can be an extension of Christ to others. Then it will reflect on the state of humanity and its own role in developing peace, justice and love in our world. It will begin afresh to face the cost of discipleship and will look for the freedom to be with Christ suffering and glorified.

MOVEMENT OF SPIRITS

A community's experiences of freedom help it to recognize spiritual desolation and consolation. This is especially important at the time of decision-making. The source of these movements can be from within the community or from beyond it. The rest of this chapter will consider those movements of spirits whose source is the interactivity among the members. These can be classified under communal desolation and communal consolation.

Movements of spirits in communal spiritual desolation

(A) FIGHTING CREATUREHOOD

Communal desolation will usually be experienced as lack of unity among the members in the face of God's presence to them. In a community's image of itself *vis-à-vis* God and others there will be a basic unwillingness to accept limitations, finiteness and dependency on God. The group might even express anger with God for the state of its being. But more often desolation will show up in the members' unwillingness to relate to each other out of vulnerability and weakness. Or 'one-upmanship' will be prevalent at the meetings; making points or winning arguments is the dominant mood. Even the prayers for help from the Lord will focus on control and independence. Among the members there will be a lack of trust, freedom, pliability, sensitivity to the action of God's grace, and readiness to respond in whatever way and direction God reveals.

(B) DENYING SINFULNESS

When the group faces its sinfulness there may be denial that the group itself is sinful. Classic statements of this are: 'Sin only exists in the will of an individual because sin demands full intentionality.' 'Sin is a failure. Why should we constantly look at failure? It is so depressing.' 'How can I be critical of this group? They are all

95

wonderful people. I joined them because they support me in my faith and I expect them to raise me up and energize me.'

In facing its sinfulness the group tends to become listless, de-energized and helpless. This tendency increases as the group becomes conscious of destructive results of its sinfulness on its own membership, other humans and the environment. Awareness of oppression and injustices within itself and beyond itself can truly be devastating to a group that wishes to bring gospel values to humanity. The knowledge of its propensity for evil can bring about a tendency to self-destruction.

In fact we know and experience that a community can be much more evil and violent in carrying out evil actions than the sum total of the group's individual sins and actions. The horrendous action of the Holocaust in Nazi Germany from 1930 to 1945 is a prime, if extreme, example of this. It was a crowd shouting 'Crucify him!' that overwhelmed the Roman representative of justice (cf. Mk 15:14). A more ordinary example might be the oppression of members of minority groups by the larger society of which they are a part. We also see this within a group when the majority ostracizes a person who proves disagreeable in discussions and commitments. As the group becomes aware that it is potentially more destructive as a group than the sum total of the members' sins it can fall into despair about itself and want to break up. People may begin to miss meetings.

As it seeks freedom from disorder and sinfulness a group may become aware of disorder on the level of unconscious projections and hidden tendencies. Among these may be racist, antisemitic, clerical, and male chauvinistic tendencies which get expressed in various jokes and snide remarks. Such awarenesses can bring two experiences of desolation: the obvious one of discouragement and pessimism, and the more subtle desolation of persons excusing themselves and escaping from responsibility.

(c) REFUSING THE CALL OF RESPONSIBILITY

If a community is able to persevere through the desolations brought about by reflecting on its communal sin history and if it is given the consolation of freedom from and with its sinfulness, it still has to face the desolations that can come as it considers a call to do something for or with Christ.

Desolation at this time will show itself in individuals' refusal to co-operate with the community in going through a discernment process to identify goals, objectives and programmes. Besides the natural objections to the work involved and to careful listening to each other there are more important signs of desolation. A community may dwell in the awareness of its limitedness and sinfulness and consider itself too small and sinful for the task of assisting Christ in the building of a better world. People's expressions may run along discouraging lines: 'We haven't even got it together ourselves. How can we help others?'

With further consideration of ways in which it might give itself to this work it can feel overwhelmed by the task before it and commitment disappears. Its previous failures come home to haunt it. Then it can refuse the call to be responsible and it takes refuge in prayers that suggest that God will do it without them: 'After all, it is God's world. God can work miracles.'

Desolation may set in when the group looks back at previous decisions. It may give up because of past failures, or refuse to evaluate actions as a way of reaching better recommendations and decisions. Spiritually, the group is denying the possibility of growth in the Lord.

(D) DESOLATION FROM EXAGGERATION AND EXUBERANCE

Another form of desolation shows itself in exaggerated enthusiasm and sense of self-importance. Initially the group may be energized by the possibilities it comes up with. It may even go through a good decision-making process with a fair amount of peace and eagerness, but then experience dissipation of energy and commitment in the implementation stage. This will be dealt with more fully later.

The communal consolation of spiritual freedom

(A) RESPONSE TO CALL IN CREATUREHOOD AND SINFULNESS

Communal consolation is characterized by acceptance of the creaturehood, dependency and limitations of the group itself and of its
need for God from within and beyond itself; a sense of newness
from the experience of being forgiven and forgiving; an energy to
reach out to others beyond the community even while experiencing
limitedness and sinfulness; and a desire to accompany Christ in his
love for humanity to the extent of suffering and dying for all humans
both good and evil.

What this means interiorly for a group is a sense of being known
and loved as it is. This is given to the community as it moves
through conscious awareness of limitedness, sinfulness and disorder
to get in touch with the unconscious forces at play in each individual
and in the community itself as well as those that come from the
culture and the human condition. Along with this affective knowledge the community experiences a sense of being carried by a power
greater than itself – in the Trinity, the communion of saints, the
human race and the church. The community is given a realistic
hope for the future.

Sometimes the consolation of freedom includes the experience of
an intellectual component: a gift of insight into its benevolent as
well as its discordant tendencies, as it evaluates its interchange and
actions. Such an affective spiritual knowledge brings the freedom
to seek forgiveness and to proceed into the future beside Christ
regardless of limitations and sinfulness and to acknowledge grate-
fully those tendencies the community realizes are altruistic.

The pain of recognition of sin brings the community to an awareness that this itself is a suffering with Christ. Jesus seemed to have
this experience of sinfulness, although he committed no sins as an
individual human being (cf. Heb 4:15). Something of this sort seems
to be the backdrop when he insists on undergoing baptism from
John the Baptist: 'John tried to dissuade him, with the words "It
is I who need baptism from you, and yet you come to me!" But
Jesus replied, "Leave it like this for the time being; it is fitting that
we should, in this way, do all that uprightness demands" ' (Mt

3:14, 15). St Paul also speaks this way: 'For our sake God made the sinless one a victim for sin, so that in Christ we might become the uprightness of God' (2 Co 5:21). The church and each Christian community experiences the cross of this awareness of suffering from sinfulness.

(B) FREEDOM FROM FEAR, SIN, INORDINATE ATTACHMENT

When a community is experiencing spiritual freedom it may experience realistic fear as it faces the future, but this fear does not cripple it. The community can now deal with exaggerated attachments and fear of physical suffering and death under the standard of the cross and resurrection of Jesus Christ. The sense of being with Christ risen as it is called into the future relativizes every possibility. The perspective of the cross and resurrection frees the community from excessive fear and opens up the community to new possibilities, which may include difficulties and suffering. The cost of discipleship no longer debilitates.

In the gospels and in the lives of the saints we are made aware that people can move through fear and be given a freedom to face suffering and death. They do this in terms of the example of Christ in hope of their own resurrection. Some persons and communities in our world have to face this very eventuality in their daily lives. They need a special strength from the Lord to persist in their struggle for justice and peace.

Fear of suffering and death can be very debilitating for a community. In some way the community has to face these possibilities and pray for freedom from these fears. The suffering and death many communities face is not as directly physical as the suffering and death of martyrs or of the poor in such a place as Central America. For communities in more comfortable circumstances, the primary fear is rather the breakup of the community. This fear can skew the life of a community. It can prevent the members from living open, honest, authentic lives.

This fear can manifest itself in different ways. People may not give full and open accounts of their actions, nor be honestly critical of each other's actions. People do not say it the way it is. A community may be passive before a member who is dominating it, for the sake of staying together. Members may be reluctant to promote a simpler life-style. Members do not encourage the community to make sacrifices for the betterment of society. Sometimes members do not reveal their doubts. They may keep some of their faith practices secret for fear of being separated. Real disagreements are not addressed for the sake of peace at all costs. The tone of the meetings can be too nice and so members are not permitted to speak about their inner turmoil of life in the parish and church. Sometimes people actually refuse to listen to such disturbance with statements like 'Everything is all right', 'We have to carry our cross'. Obviously, such fears can also prevent a community from dealing with commitments to change unjust structures in the larger society.

Eventually, the community accepts its powerlessness and radical helplessness in the face of its sinfulness and becomes conscious that God is carrying it in this state. The community has the realization of St Paul: 'Who will rescue me from this body doomed to death? God – thanks be to God – through Jesus Christ our Lord' (Rm 7:24, 25). It is given an experience of the consolation of freedom as it recognizes its new identity – that of a developing, unfinished community constantly being saved and in need of ongoing salvation.

In Romans 5 St Paul suggests that Christ as a corporate person is the new head of the human race, another Adam. In terms of this imagery the community will accept that it is a corporate person with the inclinations of the first Adam. It will wish to evolve from the unaccepting, self-justifying, fearful, irresponsible first Adam to the open, concerned, loving last Adam.

(c) FREEDOM FOR OTHERS

While some of the experiences of the consolation of freedom are a sense of release from fears and needs, others are experiences of attachment. The freeing movement beyond self that takes place when falling in love is a good expression of this. So a community may be drawn beyond itself to the sufferings of others and discover in the others the person of Christ. In the decision-making process suggested in this book this freedom is primary. It is the experience of attachment to the person of Christ that becomes the basic experience for judging other spiritual consolations at the time of decision-making.

COMING TO FREEDOM

Freedom with sinfulness and one's identity

There are a number of ways that a group can foster or encourage its sense of identity and develop grace-filled freedom. These all require the desire to establish grace-filled ways of relating within the group and the desire to be an instrument of God's grace in the world. They will involve reflection on the ways in which the group interacts and does its apostolic action. They will bring the group to state where it finds itself regarding these matters and what it desires to do for the future.

Reflecting on its past relationships in terms of its basic vision and desire may result in the graced experience of embarrassment and confusion when the community realizes that it is still in existence even though it has lived out the common experience of other groups. It may be given the intimate understanding that any group of persons which organizes itself for the good of its members or for the good of others beyond it has an innate tendency to become bad for its own members and for those it is to serve. Further reflection and sharing may bring sorrow and tears as the group realizes what it has done to its own membership and neglected to do for others.

The oppression and injustices within the group are usually more immediately obvious than faults towards those outside. But members may eventually recognize what their corporate sinfulness has done to the larger body of Christ. Shame and confusion, sorrow and tears may come as the group recognizes how far it has moved or is moving away from its potential spirit and charism. It may recognize how as an institution it has been unwilling to accept the incarnation in its midst, that is, in the limitations of its human members. Eventually the group realizes it has not reached the stage of self-destruction even though such have been its tendencies. In this experience it can pray with the whole church, 'Look not on our sins but on the faith of your church!'

The group is amazed and grateful as it becomes aware that the energy of its origins and history is still operating even though it has given its initial vision and dreams many wounds. It may be given a faith-filled knowledge of the sustaining and creative power of the larger faith community which continues to be present even though the group is not responding to graces given. Through prayerful reflection followed by sharing of the results of this individual reflection the group is led to spiritual knowledge that brings abhorrence of its shortcomings and failures on the levels of its interior group life, its apostolic actions and its succumbing to the values of the world.

Three important questions

Recalling its sinful history to discover sinful patterns in three areas will be helpful. First, how has it abused the gifts of the group? As it looks at its own style of living the group might become aware of tendencies to scapegoat, avoid serious decisions and rationalize its activity. Members may have encouraged individualism or exaggerated their gifts and limitations. The group may come to see how fragmentation, divisiveness, disempowerment, oppressive and inhuman structures have hurt it. It will help if the group does an inventory of behaviours and attitudes within itself which are sinful, for example, avoidance of painful confrontations or cutting off other persons in the midst of statements.

How have its disordered tendencies entered into its apostolic endeavour? An inventory of its internal structures and recognition of unexamined policies may be helpful as the group, for example, faces the effects of its disordered tendencies in the apostolate. The group should make an effort to bring to light its hidden assumptions, irrational ideas and disordered attachment to structures, and to move on to examine issues in the light of consequences and reasoning.

Third, how has it succumbed to the principles of the world in its decision-making and actions? As the group considers the ways in which disordered principles enter its decision-making it may recognize tendencies to workaholism and overemphasis on problem-solving and efficiency. A discussion in which each person states her or his assumptions can follow.

Discussing questions such as What's dying? What's rising? What's shaping our world? can free the community to recognize any disordered principles out of which it may be acting. A reflection on such negative signs of the times as avarice, arrogance and abuse of power might heighten awareness of the same tendencies within the group.

The group can profit greatly by considering the ways in which it has experienced and could experience 'hell' in its own life. It would do well to consider the payoffs it gets from experiences of desolation. The group might consider what would be the experience of total chaos in its membership and why this has not happened. In such a consideration the group needs to own the state of rebellion and recognize where it has lost touch with its identity and its original myth. The group might also wish to draw a negative portrait of how it would look if its compulsive tendencies and basic vices were allowed free reign.

Gaining freedom to be God's instrument

After reflecting on the various levels of sinfulness and disorder it is important that the group go through a formal reconciliation. It should seek reconciliation among its own members, reconciliation with its larger affiliation, reconciliation with the faith community beyond it, and reconciliation with the whole of humanity. Such reconciliation will involve the awareness both of sinful actions committed and of good actions omitted. Some sort of suitable penance of prayer and action ought to be performed. Restitution should be considered. Another look at the original vision, dream and desire of the group might help it consider ways of repairing losses due to its sinful actions and omissions.

When a group is considering its sinfulness, its negative tendencies and its co-operation with disordered values, it is important that it do this in an attitude of openness and reception. This requires an initial stance of humility and expectation. While the group is gaining a heightened awareness of its sinfulness it will find itself amazed, astonished and grateful for its continued existence. It might express this (as Ignatius recommends) by conversations before Christ on the cross and with the merciful Trinity. It may experience an embarrassing confusion in the face of God's abiding love for it and, recognizing the death-dealing dimensions in its interrelating, come to awareness that only God's constant grace has prevented it from bursting apart. Such abiding patience, forgiveness, kindness and compassion stir the group to new desires and new energy, now, however, in the humble awareness of its disordered tendencies to self-aggrandizement and self-achievement. With such knowledge it can proceed further into decision-making, aware, too, that vigilance and purification are constantly needed.

A Christian faith-community will realize that the various experiences of freedom are gifts from God. It will be conscious that the freedom of creaturehood, sinfulness and call are given to it in the midst of its own grappling and life. Now it will know that its very identity as a community of faith is gift and it will be able to return to the munificence of God to sustain it. In freedom it knows that however limited, disordered and sinful it may be, it is called to be with Christ serving the human race.

EXERCISE VII: FURTHER PRAYER OVER THE COMMUNITY'S HISTORY [1]

This exercise is parallel to Exercise V on the community's light history given at the end of chapter 4.

There are five steps: a communal gathering of prayer material; prayerful reflection with the material gathered; sharing the results of this prayer; reflecting on the sharing, and a brief further sharing. The group may wish to refer to the two notes accompanying the exercise at the end of chapter 2.

Theme: Our communal graced dark history

COMMUNAL PREPARATION

Contextualizing

As a communal person we enter into the dark side of our communal graced history and our need to be forgiven corporately and to make amends.

Imaging

We place ourselves in the stream of our communal history to realize how we are present in the sinful actions of our communal person.

> Salt is a good thing. But if salt itself loses its taste, what can make it salty again? (Lk 14:34)

> Jesus Christ . . . is the sacrifice to expiate our sins, and not only ours, but also those of the whole world. (1 Jn 2:2)

The grace desired

We want and desire from the Lord a sense of sorrow as we recall the sinfulness and disorder in our communal graced history.

Pointing (in the group)

Reflect quietly for about ten minutes on the following and jot down the points that come to your mind. Then share with one another and jot down further points that impress you about our history.

- Recall the significant events of our sinful history.
  Recall the cultural setting of this history.

- Reflect on our relationships within and beyond our community and the life-style of our sinful history.
  Reflect on the way in which this sinful spirit was present and showed itself as our sinful history developed.

- What impresses me about our sinful history? Where do we need to be vigilant?

PRIVATE REFLECTION

I pray with the material generated in the Pointing, reflecting on the sinful or disordered elements of our communal history.

Recall communal events where the seven capital sins have been operative. Where have we been proud, envious, unjust, uncommunicative, avaricious, resentful, or where we have contributed to sinful social structures, been disrespectful of the environment, not entered into the political struggle? Think of events that went beyond the group, and of events experienced within the group.

Where have sins of the unconscious been present, such as projections, scapegoating, stereotyping, unwillingness to pay attention to unconscious realities?

Has there been an exaggeration of the charism and virtues of our foundation present? Has the salt lost its taste?

Which of these are continuing experiences of sinfulness and disorder? Look for patterns. When and where did these begin? How did they develop? Where do we need to be vigilant?

COMMUNAL SHARING

Private review of prayer

To prepare to share, I spend some time reflecting on what happened to me in this time of prayer, for example, significant moments; insights; different affections; experiences of consolation and desolation.

What experiences of these years are significantly present to me now? What does this arouse in me?

Sharing the fruit of prayer

The group shares the above fruits of prayer in terms of questions like these:

Which of these are continuing experiences of sinfulness and disorder? Look for patterns. When and where did these begin? How did they develop? Where do we need to be vigilant?

How has the Lord brought our group through its sinful history in the past?

What dimensions of our history both within our group and in our relationship to others are still present to us and still need forgiveness and healing?

What is the significance of the pattern of our sinful history for the future?

PRIVATE REFLECTION ON OUR GROUP SHARING

I reflect on the sharing, asking:

What did I hear? What impressed me as the others shared? What new insights did I gain? What are the inevitable consequences of the truths we have shared? Where did I experience affective harmony with the others as they spoke about our history?

We briefly tell each other what moved us as the others shared the results of their prayer.

We speak to God in appreciation and anticipation. We may express wonder at the ways God has drawn our community together, and/or gratitude that God has been with the persons and events of our history up until now, and/or openness to the directions we perceive in our history.

Colloquy

I remember the words of Christ: 'In so far as you did this to one of the least of these who are members of my family, you did it to me' (Mt. 25:40).

I place myself with my community before the suffering millions in the world today and I make petitions in answer to these questions:

- Where do I see the face of Christ today?
- What is the significance of all this suffering for our forgiveness?
- What have we done for Christ?

- What are we doing for Christ?
- What ought we to do for Christ?

NOTE

[1]Cf. *ISECP* manual, volume 1, pp. 79–80.

7

INTIMATE KNOWLEDGE OF JESUS FROM CONTEMPLATING CHRIST AMONG US

I have loved you
just as the Father has loved me.
Remain in my love.
If you keep my commandments
you will remain in my love,
just as I have kept my Father's commandments
and remain in his love.
I have told you this
so that my own joy may be in you
and your joy be complete.
This is my commandment:
love one another,
as I have loved you.
No one can have greater love
than to lay down one's life for one's friends.
You are my friends,
if you do what I command you.
I shall no longer call you servants,
because a servant does not know
the master's business;
I call you friends,
because I have made known to you
everything I have learned from my Father.

(Jn 15:9–15)

Intimacy in communal discernment[1]

I remember a communal sharing in which the group listened to the great pain one of the members was experiencing as she recalled being sexually abused by a relative as a child. The community had come to the kind of trust that allowed this woman to share her inmost self. This was a moment of grace for them: it opened up experiences of pain and suffering that the others were carrying in their inner beings.

At times members of this community revealed their anger with the male-dominated church. They wondered if they could really continue in the church as committed members. 'How could God be in such an unjust structure?' they asked.

Members were also able to express great sorrow at their infidelity to the urgings of the Spirit within them. They were filled with humility at the constant goodness of God to them and their families in spite of greed and selfishness.

They were also able to share some of their religious experiences. Members told their stories of meeting Christ in their life experiences and their prayer. One member was able to speak of a special awareness of Christ as he looked upon his child. Another told of an overwhelming experience of faith in God's love for the human race while contemplating the passion of Christ. Another was able to express the sense of being carried as a child in the arms of God.

A significant dimension for a Christian community is its growth in intimate knowledge of Jesus Christ, who is the image and source of Christian ideals, desires and hopes. When St Paul sums up his exhortation to the Philippian community in the famous words, 'Make your own the mind of Christ Jesus' (Ph 2:5), he has just spelt out this 'mind' in his summary of ideal Christian community life:

> So if in Christ there is anything that will move you, any incentive to love, any fellowship in the Spirit, any warmth or sympathy – I appeal to you, make my joy complete by being of a single mind, one in love, one in heart and one in mind. Nothing is to be done out of jealousy or vanity; instead, out of humility of mind every-

one should give preference to others, everyone pursuing not selfish interests, but those of others.

(Ph 2:1–5; cf. Ga 5:13–26; Ep 4:1–7)

Such an experience of intimacy in a community is unifying and energizing. It is an experience of the presence of Christ. Recognition of this intimacy is fundamental to the discernment process because the experience of being loved by God and responding with love to God is spiritual consolation; and this consolation is the significant criterion for judging interior affective experiences when the group is trying to make decisions and to act in agreement with the desires of God.

True discernment is based on a response to the love of God moving us as we consider a possible action. Such a response is in itself an expression of intimacy with God. The action that is being discerned will find its authenticity in our participation in this intimate love of the Trinity for humanity.

Intimacy, then, is a key element in a spirituality of action for our world. Such a spirituality implies free human beings in a freely evolving universe discovering and choosing what is to be done in accord with the Trinity's loving design. Without these experiences of intimacy gained by contemplating the life of Christ, discernment cannot bring the spirituality of action into effect.

If we start with an image of God as remote and aloof, our ideas are turned upside down as we contemplate the annunciation to Mary and the birth of Jesus. Here God is anything but aloof. The mystery of the birth of Christ reveals God as intimately and unthreateningly active and present in our world to the extent that Jesus enters into our very life experiences, with all their messiness and limitations.

We, like the apostles, are the ordinary people whom God has chosen, whom Jesus calls to develop a community of love and to proclaim the resurrection to the whole world. He re-expresses his passion within our communal experiences of suffering as we attempt to continue his work on earth. The resurrection of Christ is expressed when we realize those experiences of being lifted up with Christ by the Holy Spirit.

Like Peter and the other apostles we can experience a one-to-one intimacy with Christ. Members of a Christian community who are seeking to find God in all things will be able to grow in intimacy by sharing their stories of what had happened to them as they walked with Jesus in prayer, and how they had recognized him in their own lives.

Contemplating the presence of Jesus in the faith community fosters intimate knowledge of the Lord, and the interplay between contemplation and the discernment that depends on it helps the community to develop. Trust and acceptance increase and each member begins to sense, intuit, know and feel with the other members of the community as they share their individual stories. There is an experience of unity, beauty, truth and goodness. Like Peter at the transfiguration we can exclaim, 'Master, it is good for us to be here' (Lk 9:33).

The events in the gospels which describe the way Christ relates to the community of apostles and disciples can be contemplated by the community that is trying to take on the mind and heart of Christ. Each member has to keep in mind the grace the community is praying for – the grace to have knowledge of Christ's intimate love for this community.

What is intimacy?

In a Christian community members begin to recognize intimacy in a certain sense of well-being, energy and relatedness among them. Mutual knowledge reaches real intimacy when it involves mutual acceptance. Each one knows his or her significance for the others; the whole group knows itself as a place where God's love is at work.

So intimacy is the experience of being loved and accepted, of loving and accepting; it is a heart-felt interpersonal knowledge that embraces every dimension of life. Though intimacy is something of the spirit, yet body and psyche are involved in bringing it about, whether one looks at marriage or at friendship or indeed at all human intimacy.

All spiritual consolation has the experience of intimacy as a constitutive element, whether the individual or group experiences God as sustaining presence, as desiring to save, as forgiving love, as faithful, as friend who comforts and challenges, as healer, reconciler, source of fellowship. All such experiences flow from being loved (cf. Rm 5:6) and are sensed as energizing and creative.

It is clear that intimate knowledge is not just passive awareness, nor just 'knowing about' another. Intimate knowledge has its source in the Holy Spirit, who alone can communicate the knowledge of Jesus Christ. And the Holy Spirit desires that we obtain this intimate knowledge (Rm 10:8).

A final paradox: a person might sense himself or herself as the unique focus of God's love, and in a sense this is right: 'God loves me, as I am.' And yet we realize that God's love embraces the whole human race. It is natural to wish for God's universal and unconditional love to be focused in a person, a community, a congregation, a church; but those recognizing this love will know it as indeed unconditional and universal, even while it is particular and unique. Only for a universal lover can everyone be special.

The communal experience of intimacy

Attaining communal intimate knowledge of the Lord is a stage in the growth of Christian community, beginning as the members grow in intimacy with each other and with Christ in each other. But the community as a whole begins to sense its special relationship to Christ perhaps first in terms of its scriptural encounters with Jesus as comforting, enlightening, challenging, strengthening or calling forth the community. It learns the intimacy of the early disciples with the risen Jesus, and intimacy through sufferings like those of the early church as it tried to carry out Christ's mandate. It learns also from the whole Christian Testament that it is the Holy Spirit who enables it to cry like Jesus himself: 'Abba! Father!' (Rm 8:14–26).

Jesus' experiences of intimacy while on earth

For Jesus' own experiences of intimacy are the paradigm, above all his intimacy with the One whom he addressed as 'Abba' (dear father). The words heard at his baptism 'You are my son, the

113

beloved; my favour rests on you' (Mk 1:11), express Jesus' human experience of intimacy with God. Jesus is not some spiritualized presence of God in our world: he is the channel of God's intimacy with us, and so the new head of the human race. Salvation is not just something Jesus gives, it is also something he experiences in work, in dialogue with others, in prayer, in his own resurrection and in the experience of his body the church.

In the gospels we also see Jesus in intimate relations with others: with Mary and Joseph, with Martha and Mary and Lazarus, with Mary Magdalen; with his disciples all through his ministry but perhaps above all at the last supper, as we see in John 15. In the gospels there are moments of intimacy which look idyllic: the disciples bask in the words and company of Jesus, see his mighty deeds and even share his power. But there are discordant moments too, when they bicker among themselves over precedence; and there are moments of decision, easy perhaps at first, more painful later on. There is intimacy between Jesus and his friends in pleasant and unpleasant situations, in praise and challenge; Jesus' intimacy is such that he can call his friends to follow him with total commitment.

Intimacy in the post-resurrection faith communities

As the story of Paul's conversion shows, these intimate encounters with Jesus did not cease after the resurrection. After his meeting with Jesus on the Damascus road Paul realized that 'Jesus is Lord'. He saw the significance of the Christian community he had been trying to destroy, its union with Jesus and his own need to join it through baptism into Christ.

The intimate activity of the breaking of bread among the faithful while remembering the life, death and resurrection of Jesus becomes part of the worshipping activity of the early church. We read in Acts: 'These remained faithful to the teaching of the apostles, to the fellowship, to the breaking of bread and to the prayers' (Ac 2:42). The communal activity of breaking bread is always an experience of intimacy. Many of the post-resurrection encounters with Jesus take place in the context of a communal meal: with the two disciples at Emmaus, in the Upper Room with the apostles, by the lakeside with Peter.

In the letters of Paul we find an awareness of the intimacy of Jesus with the early church. There are numerous texts where Paul speaks of the intimacy of the membership with Christ and with each other, for example:

> Every one of you that has been baptized has been clothed in Christ. There can be neither Jew nor Greek, there can be neither slave nor free, there can be neither male nor female – for you are all one in Christ Jesus.
>
> (Ga 3:27–8)

> If we live by the truth and in love, we shall grow completely into Christ, who is the head . . . So the body grows until it has built itself up in love.
>
> (Ep 4:15–16)

As we have seen, possibly the early church's most intimate experience with Jesus is in the ability of the community to address God as Dear Father.

> You received the spirit of adoption, enabling us to cry out, 'Abba, Father!' The Spirit himself joins with our spirit to bear witness that we are children of God . . . and joint-heirs with Christ, provided that we share his suffering, so as to share his glory.
>
> (Rm 8:15–17)

As in the earthly life of Jesus so in the resurrected life of Christ there are idyllic, discordant and decision-making events within the faith community. Pentecost is the most awesome of the idyllic events, but there is also the beautiful experience of fellowship in the early church in their common prayers and sharing of goods (Ac 2:42–7). Paul's letters reveal many situations of disagreement and conflict, and the Council of Jerusalem (Acts 15) is perhaps the prime example of communal decision-making in the early church.

> 'It has been decided by the Holy Spirit and by ourselves not to impose on you any burden beyond these essentials: you are to abstain from food sacrificed to idols, from blood, from the meat

of strangled animals and from illicit marriages. Avoid these, and you will do what is right.'

(Ac 15:28–9)

This passage of scripture is a paradigm of Christian communal decision-making. A community today might often return to it prayerfully especially at a time when the community is considering a serious issue that is quite contentious.

INTIMACY WITHIN THE CHRISTIAN COMMUNITY TODAY

Communal intimacy with Christ is not only something we read about in scripture. It is happening today. A basic reason for the welling-up of so many small Christian communities today is the sense of intimacy with Christ that the members experience. It is in the prayers and interchanges of the faith community remembering and appreciating the experience of the paschal mystery that the intimacy of Jesus continues to be experienced. Contemplating Christ in the present experiences of humanity and as focused in a particular faith community is the method of heightening awareness of the presence of Christ with us. This knowledge of Christ becomes the basic experience for discerning the intimate presence of Christ to the community.

In the gospel story of Jesus' historical experience we see how he is drawn by his intimate knowledge of God to decision in the Garden of Gethsemane and to the free act of dying on the cross. So the faith community will experience the intimate presence of Christ as it discerns its decisions and actions in union with the paschal mystery of Christ.

This paschal mystery is ongoing. It is being experienced now in humanity and in each faith community. Contemplating the presence of Christ in humanity and in a faith community from this perspective gives us an intimate understanding of Christ with us and moves us forward with resolve and joy to decision and action for the betterment of all humanity.

Through communal contemplation a community can grow in

116

intimacy with the risen Christ in its midst. Intimacy will be experienced as communal spiritual consolation. It is important for the community to reflect upon these experiences to foster a sense of spiritual union and energy among the members and to heighten awareness of that unique experience of the presence of the risen Lord in the community. This is of special significance when the community is discerning decisions and actions.

All of the basic spiritualities of Christianity have insisted on the significance of the story of Jesus in our attitude towards life. This is especially true in contemplation. We return to the faith community's stories in scripture as the source of being present to our own story. A community is called to bring together the faith-memory of the church with its own story. It does this by recalling the communal stories of Jesus with his disciples and the risen Christ with the early church.

An individual or community contemplating the gospel stories might experience various states of intimacy with Christ: an idyllic state while contemplating the infancy narratives; a disturbing state when being challenged to walk on the waters with Peter; a decision state while contemplating the decision to go up to Jerusalem with Jesus; a cost-of-discipleship state while contemplating the Passion; a joyful state while contemplating the Resurrection; an ecstatic state while seeking to find God in all things and so attain the love of God.

The activity of contemplation

I am suggesting that the activity of contemplating the presence of Christ in the ongoing experience of humanity and in this faith community brings the gift of intimacy. How does a community do this? I would like to recall some of the insights and instructions about contemplation developed by St Ignatius in his *Spiritual Exercises*.

For Ignatius the activity of contemplating the mysteries of the life of Christ as presented in the gospels is the occasion for intimacy. Through such prayer the person seeks intimacy – to know God and Jesus as intimate friend and companion who evokes our deepest

117

desires and calls us forth with him. Such prayer may bring us the comforting experiences of holding a child or being held by a parent or friend, or the challenging experiences of having a prophet pointing out our sins or of having a leader call us to follow through the fire and the flood. Ignatius' instructions for persons following the Spiritual Exercises actually focus on the desire for intimacy with Jesus Christ in the grace being sought: 'Here it will be to ask for a deep interior knowledge of the Lord who has become human for me, that I may love and follow my Lord ever more closely' (Exx 104).

Praying for such a grace from God indicates that persons cannot attain it through their own efforts. Intimate knowledge of another person, in this case Jesus Christ, is always a gift. In the *Spiritual Exercises* Ignatius hopes that those praying will be given such knowledge so that they will decide and act in tune with the mind and heart of Christ.

Although Ignatius brings forth realistic material in the contemplations on the incarnation and the nativity with references to the cross and the cost of our redemption, still the experience of the one contemplating is usually one of amazement and security in the presence of these two mysteries. There is not much fear or disturbance in praying for the grace of intimate knowledge of Jesus in order to love him more dearly and follow him more closely.

Ignatian contemplation is a way of entering into mystery and receiving the sense of Christ's presence in a conscious way. It is both an experience and a method of prayer. Sometimes the experience precedes the method and sometimes the method is the occasion for the experience of presence.

Persons and communities who wish to attain an intimate knowledge of Jesus in order to make correct decisions and actions will need to use both memory and imagination, and they will do this in the context of life as a mystery to be lived rather than a problem to be solved.

The experience of mystery

When we pray according to the method of contemplation taught by St Ignatius, we focus on a particular gospel story. The good news of Jesus comes to us in narrative or story form. Stories are fascinating not only for what they say, but also for what they do not say. The imagination works in conjunction with the story if it is spoken or read and goes beyond the words heard or spoken.

Each of these events draws the one praying into the total mystery of Jesus Christ. When contemplating the birth of Jesus Ignatius gives these instructions:

> . . . see and consider what they are doing, for example, making the journey and suffering that the Lord may be born in the greatest poverty; and after so many labours, after hunger, thirst, heat, and cold, after insults and injuries, might die on the cross, and all this for me.
>
> (Exx 116)

Mystery always says something more. It is never totally contained. So it is with all the mysteries of creation, sinfulness and forgiveness, call and response. This is particularly true of Jesus Christ, God become human, of the faith community called church, of myself as person. If we approach all these subjects as mystery we take on a new attitude and see life in new perspective. Life itself becomes a discovery process. Compulsions can be handled. We pray differently. We approach discernment differently.

Explanation only enhances mystery. Reductionism cannot handle it, for in mystery the whole is greater than the sum of its parts. A person is more than a sensing, psychic, spiritual being. A person is not an isolated unity, but a being constituted by relationship, known in the context of the beyond. The response to mystery is awe, wonder, reverence, amazement and love. 'I tremble in fear and burn with love' expresses it well.

Our appreciation of mystery depends on revelation. In our human interpersonal relationships there is intimacy when one person reveals his or her interior life to another. In God–human or Christ–human relationships the mysteries of our existence, our life and our death are revealed to us by grace.

119

Mystery also implies the presence of life force, energy, something that impacts on our senses, psyche and spirit. Presence has to be recognized. Sometimes it is to be appreciated, sometimes it is to be analysed and understood, sometimes it is to be discerned. For Christians there is not only the presence of God creating and sustaining humanity, but there is also the human–divine presence of the person of Jesus Christ.

Memory

Contemplation involves a concurrence of the memory of our personal life experiences and the faith-memory of the church, which includes the memory of many centuries. The most obvious example of this concurrence is the communal work of the people, the Eucharist, accomplished through this faith-memory of the church. The gospels themselves are the memories of the early Christian communities, coloured by the resurrection experiences of the early church.

All contemplation is dependent on the communal memory present in the eucharistic action of the church. The individual can only contemplate while in a eucharistic stance to life, i.e. in the paschal mystery of Christ, even if this is not explicit. The risen Jesus and his ongoing life are the starting-point for contemplation, the entry into the mysteries of his life.

When a community wishes to contemplate and receive the intimate knowledge of Christ in its midst it will use its memory as it recalls the mysteries of Christ's life or the mystery of its own history. In the context of life as mystery, remembering gives us the awareness of Christ's experiences of intimacy with God and us. It leads us to an intimate experience of the mind and heart of Christ.

Ignatius invites those making the Spiritual Exercises to use active imagination with the gospel story. They can be present in the event by seeing the persons, hearing what they are saying, watching what they are doing and reflecting on themselves within the situation.

This active imagination is closely connected to our faith memory, that is, to the elements of our faith applied to our own life experiences. So, for example, I may have read and prayed over Jesus' words to the disciples on the way to Emmaus that 'the Christ should suffer before entering into his glory' (Lk 24: 26) and believe that this is true. Yet I may not have gut-level knowledge of this truth of the faith. But if I return to my own life experiences and recognize how Christ has brought life out of death for me, or energy out of despondency, or hope out of fear, then I will be given intimate knowledge of this truth and intimate knowledge of Jesus. The juxtaposing of the community's memory of its life experiences with the gospel story helps it to be present in the mystery and grow in intimacy with the Lord. With such intimate knowledge of Christ the community has the experience to assist it in its discerned decisions and actions.

Ways to grow in intimacy with Christ

There are a number of ways a community might be given intimacy with Christ. One is through contemplating gospel events of Christ's intimacy with his disciples. A second is a consideration of Christ's intimacy with the early church communities as presented in Acts and the apostolic letters. A third is by raising consciousness of the presence of the risen Christ in the community itself.

I. CONTEMPLATING THE GOSPEL STORIES: THE EVENT AND THE GRACE

Choosing the communal event to contemplate is important. A community might do this by getting a deep sense of their special need at the time. Then they can choose the scriptural event which is closest to their need and contemplate it in one way or another.

A community might experience such needs as: freedom among the members and the ability to deal with differences; reconciliation among the members; recognition of communal sin or sinful social structures working in themselves; generosity; vision and energy; discernment among themselves and beyond themselves; full commitment to the cross of Christ; compassion with the sufferings of others; ability to rejoice with others, or the need to find God in all things and serve God more fully.

In considering the ways a community may gain intimacy with Christ it is important to remember that the experience of intimacy with Christ is a gift. It is a grace from God. Those who seek such a grace can only dispose themselves and set up occasions for the gift to be given. The possible consequences may include the stirring up of great fear; members must be willing and open to have such experiences. The community will have to pray fervently for a sense of intimacy with Christ as it contemplates.

1. One process for contemplating gospel events might be the following: (a) Members contemplate a communal event of Jesus with his disciples. (b) Members share results of their contemplations. (c) The community compares the intimacy given in the contemplations with its own experience of intimacy.

2. Another process is a) to ask each member to assume the place of a disciple and then enter the contemplation as that disciple. b) The members come together and share their contemplations of being one of the disciples. c) The community then shares the impact of listening to the others.

3. A third way of gaining intimate knowledge of Christ would begin with a communal preparation of points for prayer from some communal scene of the Christian Testament. After this the members would pray privately with the points seeking to realize Christ's intimate way of relating to communities. The fruits of this prayer are shared with the rest of the community. The community then opens itself up to an experience of Christ's intimacy with itself as a Christian community.[2]

4. A fourth way for the community to come to this intimacy with Christ is to use one of the events of the gospels and by means of questions and answers to raise consciousness of the parallels between these events and the community's own historical experience of Christ in its midst.

2. CONTEMPLATING THE PRESENCE OF THE RISEN CHRIST IN THE
ACTS OF THE APOSTLES AND THE APOSTOLIC LETTERS

There are events in the Acts that can be contemplated in ways similar to those with the gospels. However, now we are forced to see, hear and watch the impact of the risen Christ in the minds and hearts of the apostles. The Spirit of Christ is known by the activity of the Christians. So we see a certitude in Peter that indicates the presence of Christ: 'I have neither silver nor gold, but I will give you what I have: in the name of Jesus Christ the Nazarene, walk!' (Ac 3:6)

Contemplating events in the apostolic letters requires that we move into the very mind and heart of the author. This might be done by bringing a passage of Paul, Peter, James, John or Jude before the community and letting the author be present to indicate its meaning for the community. The community might then reflect and share what it saw, heard and understood.

3. CONTEMPLATING THE COMMUNITY'S OWN MYSTERY

1. A community can gain a sense of the Lord's intimacy with it by reflecting on the very giftedness and sufferings of the members. They can express their awareness of Jesus in their community, by sharing the gifts, virtues and beatitudes of the various members of the community. They will seek the grace to recognize the immediate presence of Christ among them. Such contemplations begin with the insight of Paul: 'All of us, however, reflect the glory of the Lord with uncovered faces; and that same glory coming from the Lord who is the Spirit, transforms us into his very likeness, in an ever greater degree of glory' (2 Co 3:18, *Good News Bible*). Each member might reflect quietly for some time on the gift that every other person brings to her or him and then share with the others how they find Paul's statement is true for everyone. After sharing the group might contemplate some more the presence of Christ in the group. This kind of spiritual exercise could cover many sessions.

2. The community can return to the exercises of praying on its graced history and enter again into the experiences of God's presence and faithfulness (see chapters 4 and 6). Through group sharing the community will be able to appreciate more fully God's activity in its life, whether it was lightsome, dark, sinful, challenging, suffering or joy-filled. This becomes contemplation as the members see and hear and touch in faith memory the persons in the history, the

123

state of the world during this history, and the various activities the group has performed. During such contemplation the group may make acts of gratitude, wonder and appreciation of God's Spirit with it during this history.

3. Another way for the community to contemplate the mystery of itself is the community's history line. This is also a way for members of a community to dispose themselves for the spiritual knowledge of Christ's intimacy with them. After creating the communal history line as explained in chapter 5, the community can sit in front of it and remember within the presence of the risen Christ the decisive events with their emotional impact and meanings, paying special attention to how they have experienced the paschal mystery of Christ, his life, death and resurrection.

EXERCISE VIII. INTIMATE KNOWLEDGE OF JESUS FROM CONTEMPLATING CHRIST AMONG US

Intimate knowledge of Jesus Christ among us can be gained if we become aware of the spiritual gifts among the members of the community. Recognizing and acknowledging these gifts is a way to contemplate Christ's presence to the community. Being present to the community's history line also helps the group to contemplate Christ's faithfulness to the community.

Contextualizing

All of us then, reflect the glory of the Lord with uncovered faces; and that same glory, coming from the Lord who is the Spirit, transforms us into his very likeness, in an ever greater degree of glory. (2 Co 3:18, *Good News Bible*)

Imaging

We image ourselves as an extension of the risen Lord in the world.

The grace desired

We pray for an intimate knowledge of Christ among us that we might discern our decisions and actions for humanity.

Pointing

I recall events in our communal history.

I recall the sharing of our basic dream, vision and hopes as a Christian faith community.

I spend some time contemplating each member of my community, seeing them, hearing them, watching what they are doing, looking for the intimate presence of Christ in each one of them. I open my mind and heart to recognize the special gifts each one brings to the community.

Colloquy

We share with each other what we saw and heard and touched. We make appropriate acts of thanks and hope to Christ. We end with the *Lord's Prayer*.

EXERCISE IX: A COMMUNAL CONTEMPLATION OF A COMMUNAL GOSPEL EVENT

There are different ways for a community to use the following exercise.

a. Each member can pray through the week on the mystery presented, reflect on the experience of this prayer and come prepared to share with the community what happened in prayer. At the meeting the results of prayer are shared and the community reflects on and shares what has been given to it in the sharing.

b. The community can do a common prayer period on this event at one sitting. After a brief time in the presence of the scriptural material, persons can relate what they saw and heard and the feelings this raised in them. Then the members can spend some more silent time reflecting on what this means for the community. Where do they sense Christ's intimacy with them as community? What does this mean for their own interaction?

c. The community may begin with (b). Then through the week each member might pray on the mystery presented, reflect on the experience of this prayer and come prepared to share with the community what happened in prayer. At the meeting the results of prayer are shared and the community reflects on and shares what has been given to it in the sharing.

CONTEMPLATION OF THE MULTIPLICATION OF THE LOAVES AND FISHES

Contextualizing

The apostles rejoined Jesus and told him all they had done and taught, and he said to them, 'Come away to some lonely place all by yourselves and rest for a while'; for there were so many coming and going that there was no time for them even to eat. So they set off in the boat to a lonely place where they could be by themselves. But people saw them going, and many recognized them; and from every town they all hurried to the place on foot and reached it before them. So as he stepped ashore he saw a large crowd; and he took pity on them because they were like sheep without a shepherd, and he set himself to teach them at some length. By now it was getting very late, and his disciples came up to him and said, 'This is a lonely place and it is getting very late, so send them away, and they can go to the farms and villages round about, to buy themselves something to eat.' He replied, 'Give them something to eat yourselves.' They answered, 'Are we to go and spend two hundred denarii on bread for them to eat?' He asked, 'How many loaves have you? Go and see.' And when they had found out they said, 'Five, and two fish'. Then he ordered them to get all the people to sit down in groups on the green grass, and they sat down on the ground in squares of hundreds and fifties. Then he took the five loaves and the two fish, raised his eyes to heaven and said the blessing; then he broke the loaves and began handing them to his disciples to distribute among the people. He also shared out the two fish

126

among them all. They all ate as much as they wanted. They collected twelve basketfuls of scraps of bread and pieces of fish. Those who had eaten the loaves numbered five thousand. (Mk 6:30–44)

Imaging

We image ourselves as disciples of the Lord among the apostles as we share this incident with Jesus.

The grace desired

We ask of God an intimate knowledge of the way Jesus Christ relates to us as community so that we can better love and serve communally God's concerns for the whole human race.

Points

Reflect and share on the following:

Whom do you see present: Jesus, the disciples, the multitude, ourselves? Hear them speak of the difficulties and successes of their mission. Hear Jesus' voice as he speaks to them. What is its tone?

How does Jesus speak to the multitude? How does he call on the apostles to help him? How does he speak to us on this occasion?

How do we speak to each other in this event? How do we listen to the Lord? What do we see Jesus and the apostles doing? What are we doing? What would we like to do? How do we carry on our mission? How do we feed the multitude? How was Christ intimate with the disciples and the crowd? How was Christ intimate with us?

After the sharing, further reflection and sharing:

How were we in the event? Who did we speak and listen to? What did we do? What impressed you as others shared? What do you sense took place in the group?

Colloquy

We speak to the Lord about his intimacy with the disciples. We speak to each other about the Lord's intimacy with us. We end with the *Lord's Prayer*.

EXERCISE X: SHARING PERSONAL CONTEMPLATIONS ON THE VARIOUS APPEARANCES OF THE RESURRECTED CHRIST.[3]

This exercise is done in the following way:

1. A discussion coordinator asks different members to enter the gospel event as one of the persons experiencing the risen Lord.

2. Members contemplate the event before sharing.

3. In the context of the Upper Room on Easter Sunday night the members share their experiences of meeting the risen Lord in the contemplations.

- One member contemplates Mk 16:1–8 as Salome.
  2nd member contemplates Mk 16:1–8 as Mary the
     mother of James.
  3rd member contemplates Jn 20:11–17 as Mary Magdalen.
  4th member contemplates Jn 20:1–10 as John.
  5th member contemplates Jn 20:1–10 as Peter.
  6th member contemplates Lk 24:12, 34 as Peter alone.
  7th member contemplates Lk 24:13–27 as Cleopas.
  8th member contemplates Lk 24:13–27 as Mary, Cleopas' wife.

- Each person enters the gospel event by using their imagination to see the persons, hear what they are saying and watch what they are doing and reflecting on themselves to draw some profit. They are continually intent on seeking what they want and desire of God, that is, intimate understanding of the Lord risen for our sake that we may the better love and follow him.

- When next the group gathers together they continue with the following activity of communal memory.

AN EXERCISE OF COMMUNAL MEMORY

Contexualizing

The disciples set out that instant and returned to Jerusalem. There they found the Eleven assembled together with their companions, who said to them, 'The Lord has indeed risen and has appeared to Simon.' Then they told their story of what had happened on the road and how they had recognized him at the breaking of bread. (Lk 24:33–5)

Imaging

The group images itself as disciples of the Lord sharing their experiences of the risen Christ.

The grace desired

We ask of God an intimate knowledge of the way Jesus Christ relates to us as community so that we can better love and serve communally God's concerns for the whole human race.

Points

Small group sharing:
Be with the disciples in the Upper Room on Easter night. Each person shares the experience of contemplation each had as Magdalen, Peter . . . etc.

Reflection after the sharing:
Reflect on the small group experience for three minutes:
- What impressed you as the others shared?
- What do you sense took place in your own group?

Further sharing:
Share in small groups for twelve minutes your reflections on the two questions.

129

Complete the exercises by reading Luke 24:36–43.

They were still talking about all this when he himself stood among them and said to them, 'Peace be with you!' In a state of alarm and fright, they thought they were seeing a ghost. But he said, 'Why are you so agitated, and why are these doubts stirring in your hearts? See by my hands and my feet that it is I myself. Touch me and see for yourselves; a ghost has no flesh and bones as you can see I have.' And as he said this he showed them his hands and his feet. Their joy was so great that they still could not believe it, as they were dumbfounded; so he said to them, 'Have you anything here to eat?' And they offered him a piece of grilled fish, which he took and ate before their eyes. (Lk 24:36–43)

Colloquy

We speak to the Lord about his intimacy with the disciples. We speak to each other about the Lord's intimacy with us. We end with the *Lord's Prayer*.

NOTES

[1] 'The relationship between God and ourselves is not . . . confrontational. It is an invitation to loving encounter, intimacy, love, communion, and oneness, as chapters 14 and 15 of the Gospel of John so beautifully attest' (Dick Westley: *Redemptive Intimacy, A New Perspective for the Journey to Adult Faith* (Twenty Third Publications, Mystic, CT, 7th printing 1989), p. 99).
[2] See Exercise IX below, pp. 125–8.
[3] This exercise comes from the Experienced Spiritual Directors' Seminar 'Making New Wineskins: From the individual to the community: the challenge of spiritual directors today', held at Loyola House, Guelph, Ontario, in February 1989.

THE DISCERNMENT PROCESS OF A COMMUNITY OF DISCIPLES

God is not the mastermind of a vast construction activity, planned in computerised fashion from the beginning and moving on inevitably to a predetermined and preconceived end . . . This mysterious Artist is committed in passion, righteousness and holiness to an infinite creative activity, launched by love and seeking, making and feeling its way forward by freedom and in freedom . . . Nothing is certain, but everything is possible. Such committed and constructive openness is the basic condition of freedom and love.

(Bishop David Jenkins) [1]

A SPIRITUALITY OF RESPONSIBLE ACTION

Most of our deliberation on the discernment process of a small faith community has looked at internal workings. We have seen how a group can learn to recognize and foster a spiritual atmosphere conducive to good decisions. We have considered some of the ways in which the group will grow in its ability to share, in open-mindedness to possible actions, and even in its willingness to suffer. We have seen how discernment serves as an instrument to bring about a sense of communal identity, and how the continuing process of communal discernment can assist a community to grow and become an agent of God's goodness and love in our world. It is time, therefore, to shift our attention from the inner life of the community to the interface between it and the world outside.

This is the place for realism. We live in a developing world moving through disorders to order. As the community considers how it wants to serve as co-creators in a positive constructive way it has to remember that, just as in the inner life of the group, so in its experience of the larger world, it encounters both true and deceptive ideologies and energies. There is good and evil in both spheres. In looking for a spirituality of responsible action, we are acknowledging that people are worthwhile, that human history has a goal, and that meaning and value are not confined to our religion and our church.

Image of a responsible community

As a community considers the challenges from outside forces upon it, it begins to ask questions about its encounters with freedom and responsibility.

As its root meaning suggests, responsibility involves the ability to respond to someone or something. This in turn implies that someone or something is impinging on our being, urging us and calling us forth, sometimes comfortingly, and sometimes disturbingly.

In accepting freedom and responsibility toward others a community may have to become open to change in some of its basic images. These include images of God's being and the way God relates to each person and to the various communities of human beings. They also include images of ourselves and the ways we relate to God and our world and of the place of the world in our spirituality.

Freedom

Particularly when considering our response to energies from outside, we are challenged to become conscious of the images we have of the will of God and of our freedom in this world as well as our image of human interaction.

We can never plumb the full depths of the mystery of God's freedom and our freedom. Yet we can get in touch with some aspects of an image of the will of God that will foster our free response. Humans are in a free relationship with each other and

132

with God. 'There are many different gifts, but it is always the same Spirit; and there are many different ways of serving, but it is always the same Lord. There are many different forms of activity, but in everybody it is the same God who is at work in them all' (1 Co 12:4–6). We make our decision freely, yet in response to grace already moving us to take responsibility and act. The heuristic (or discovery) dimension in discernment is not discovering the will of God in the already-out-there-now-real, but discerning the forward movement of our free life force in relation to the human condition and God's presence and continuous act of creation.

Discernment, of course, presupposes that our universe is set up in such a way that God is free and not controlled by eternal laws which God is bound to fulfil. This is a great mystery for us. Discernment also presupposes that we are not limited to a process of deducing from eternal laws what God's will is for our decisions. We can discover the desires of God through an inductive process which combines a reading of the signs of the times coming out of a social consciousness and discernment of the movement of spirits in our interior being in relation to any particular situation or opportunity.[2]

A deductive approach would be somewhat like working through a detective story in which we attempted to put all the pieces together so that we could know definitively what is already in place. Or it might be compared to a scientific experiment in which we attempted to find all the variables and deduce an answer to the problem we are working on. All we would need is a large enough computer so that the variables could be entered into the formula. Such approaches to spiritual discernment eventually break down.

The inductive process works from a position of freedom. We must consider the freedom of God and the God of freedom. We can avoid our responsibility by resorting to our ignorance of God's freedom. We might admit that God must be free, but God is such a mystery that we cannot totally fathom God's freedom. And this is true. However, it is our operative image that is important here. Do we really operate as if God can act freely in the created universe and as if God promotes our responsible freedom?

Do we believe that we are free? Do we sense that our free decisions and actions make any difference in our universe? Or as we think and act do we adjust to a set of predetermined laws that we think must underlie our universe?

The idea that we live in a free universe with free responsible beings in it suggests that our free decisions and actions are significant to the human race and to God and that God goes with our decisions and actions. We are the ones who make history by our decisions and actions. We are responsible for the building of God's realm of peace, justice and love in our world. Yet we are not alone. The Spirit of God is assisting us with insight, courage and love to decide and act for the betterment of humanity.

The image of ourselves as co-creators with God means that our prayer becomes orientated toward seeking guidance from God over concrete historical decisions and actions. In our communal discerning process we also need to promote the free commitment of all the members as we work to decisions and actions.[3] In communal discernment the authority resides in all members of the community and not in one or another person who might be designated as president, leader or coordinator. All forms of oppression, whether due to authority, prophetic ability, superior physical strength, masculinism, femininism or intellectual expertise, automatically invalidate the discernment. This is not to deny the significance of authority, prophecy, the physical, the masculine, the feminine or intellectual expertise in discernment, provided they are not used oppressively. Free consensus of both free minds and free hearts is the only atmosphere in which communal discernment can take place.

There are forces impinging on a small faith community that can move it to decisions and actions that are beneficial to the human race or detrimental to the human race. These have to be discerned. No small Christian faith community is a law unto itself. It exists within the ambience of the larger faith community known as church and within the whole human family. Its decisions and actions are the result of this interrelationship with the larger church and humanity and affect the larger church and humanity. To some extent this truth always has to be considered in the discernment process. One of the small community's desires at the time of deciding is to 'feel with the church' in an attitude of love and trust. It will look to this larger faith community to confirm its decisions before going into action. So it recognizes the importance of its decisions and actions for the church and humanity at large.

In this state a community moves to an image of itself as a ministerial group. While it may always consider itself as sinful and wounded and in need of forgiveness and healing it may now picture itself as a group of disciples of the Lord. With this image a new identity starts to take shape and new elements in its decision-making process have to be considered.

The group may have shared many experiences by this time: faith-sharing experiences of healing and acceptance, limitedness and sinfulness, identity and recognition, freedom and call, consolation and desolation, and intimacy with Christ. The group has learned how to listen to and express its deep interior life. It has learned how to support and encourage, how to accept and challenge. It has learned the significance of its light and shadow history for an understanding of itself. It has learned how to receive consolations and desolations arising in its own internal interchanges. It has learned how to contemplate as a community – over its own history or with the stories of the early church as given in the gospels, Acts and the apostolic letters.

Now as a community of disciples in the Lord it will see communal responsibility as an act of stewardship for the world beyond it. It has attained a stance of openness and interior freedom among the members of the community but is aware of its larger role *vis-à-vis* humanity. In its new sense of itself it desires to discern its apostolic response.

It will discover that there are two sources of energy moving it to fulfil its role as a community of disciples. The first is from within its own membership and the second is from beyond. These two interrelate. But discernment is over the movements within the community whether they began from within or from beyond it.

As it follows its apostolic desires the community will need two things: a growing intimacy with Christ as a community of disciples and knowledge of the ways various forces from beyond impinge upon it as decisions approach.

A NEW STAGE OF DISCERNMENT

Discerning forces from within the community

When a community recognizes that it is called by the Lord to go beyond itself, it will have certain interior movements, some debilitating and some invigorating. It could quite easily become frightened, back off and not commit itself. Some members might leave as did some of Jesus' disciples after the multiplication of the loaves and fishes. It was after this event that Jesus announced: 'Whoever eats my flesh and drinks my blood lives in me and I live in that person' (Jn 6:56). Or the group might leave the Lord's call in sadness as did the rich young man who had many possessions (cf. Lk 18:18–23).

On the other hand the community might experience magnanimity and desire to do the greater thing for God. No doubt the apostles experienced spiritual consolation as they received the Lord's commission and went off in enthusiasm to proclaim the good news (cf. Lk 9:1–16). They were in tune with the Lord's wishes and carried by his love to become instruments of grace for others.

But this outward orientation of spiritual consolation can also be an occasion for deception, for deception can take place when we are in a high energy state of good will towards others, as happens when we are in a generous mood or excited by insights. At such times we can make decisions out of the exciting energy rather than for the sake of God's reign. Careful discernment is necessary to recognize the motivation moving us to decision and action.

With this outward orientation the community also faces powers from beyond the group that influence its decisions and actions. Now it realizes it has come to a new phase of discernment. It will need to discern the ways these outside forces interact with its interior life and move it to decisions that can be beneficial or destructive to itself and through it to the world at large.

136

Discerning forces exterior to the community

As a preliminary to such discernment the community will seek an experiential knowledge of how outside forces impinge on its life and decision-making for good or evil. It can gain a heightened awareness of this by reflecting on the ways they affect its physical, psychological and spiritual self. It will search to know if the external influences are leading it to fulfil its authentic mission in life or leading it into deception.

Sometimes the community is threatened and at other times attracted by these forces. They may clash or harmonize with its interior state. Both experiences need to be discerned. Those forces the community finds threatening may be an indication of call or challenge. Those it finds attractive may be deceptive. At this stage in a community's development analysis of the immediate experience is not enough. The community needs to consider the whole train of thoughts and affective movements that it has experienced over time while considering a particular issue. It may discover a pattern of experience, thought and decision that has led to wrong or less good actions. On the other hand, it may discover a pattern of experience, thought and decision that has led to good or better actions. This investigating of patterns of influence from outside forces on us is described in the Second Week Rules of Discernment (cf. Exx 332–5).

A community can judge these two movements in terms of the patterns given by St Ignatius in the Two Standards Meditation (cf. Exx 142, 146). He suggests that both movements begin with experiences that appear good. However, they move towards different ends, one to a bad or less good end, the other to a good or better end. The first is deceptive, turning us from our deep desires. The other is true, keeping us on course with our deep desires.

Ignatius suggests that a deceptive pattern begins with an appeal to an apparent good, namely riches, which then lead to honour and pride. The authentic pattern begins with an apparent evil, namely poverty, which then leads to humiliations and humility. The deceptive pattern has been recognized down the ages by sages and prophets of all cultures. The authentic pattern is based on the teaching and example of Christ, although it seems to run against human nature and can only be accepted with the help of God's grace.

Deceptive patterns[4]

For a community to discern whether the spiritual consolation it is experiencing is authentic or deceptive it needs reflective knowledge of the ways it is usually called forth authentically and the ways it is usually deceived. It gains this by looking for patterns of authentic call and patterns of deception. Such patterns are experienced communally (as well as individually) in very subtle ways. No evil angel appears before us grandly suggesting that we will be the great saviours of the world, and then leading us to destructive decisions and actions.

Initially, a community might begin its process of discovering deceptive patterns by considering the ways that deceptive patterns are present in today's world. It might reflect on the reasons our culture rewards people for their activities. For example, notice the ways our culture rewards people for overwork, intelligence or good looks: more money, more prestige, leading to exotic foods, nice clothing, larger houses, expensive recreation and entertainment.

Reflecting on the substance- and process-addictive elements in our society (smoking, alcohol, drugs, overeating, sex, constant need for excitement in entertainment and recreation, shopping and spending money, workaholism, power and control) can give us insights and helps to recognize such patterns in our communal life, for the small community will tend to imitate the larger cultural movements. Another way of getting in touch with deceptive patterns is to study the deceptive patterns in such domains as the sports world, the entertainment world, big business, big government and big church.

A community, like individuals, can investigate the ways that talents, gifts and virtues get exaggerated in various interchanges and actions. Members may notice that they always tend to be nice or never to confront. They may find the group tends to place a premium on being brilliant in discussion. While people should be affirmed, a community may give inordinate adulation of individual efforts. An outsider would recognize the phoniness in the situation.

A community must be vigilant against adopting deceptive patterns which may flow from the surrounding culture into its behaviour. For example, members may find that they are reflecting on decisions with a conviction that they must win at any cost. Or they may find themselves gradually adopting certain modes of dress which are aimed at attaining recognition. These patterns tend to creep into their beliefs without anyone noticing. Other problematic patterns could include beliefs in bureaucratic control, efficiency, lobbying, and such assumptions as 'the rules will keep you', as well as the belief that we do well to sacrifice the individual for the common good, or the notion that the Beatitudes suggest passivity and non-involvement.

Authentic patterns

Authentic patterns are those which concur with the values and style of life proclaimed by the Christian scriptures. From the viewpoint of interior movements of spirit these will show up in attitudes and experiences of the community. The community might reflect carefully on the patterns of true call given in the writing of the early church. For example, Jesus says to his apostles:

> Anyone who comes to me without hating father, mother, wife, children, brothers, sisters, yes, and even life itself, cannot be my disciple. No one who does not carry the cross and come after me can be my disciple.
>
> (Lk 14:26–7)

St Paul expresses this in a prayer: '. . . that I may come to know Christ and the power of his resurrection, and partake of his sufferings by being moulded to the pattern of his death' (Ph 3:10). St Ignatius sums up Christ's instructions to his disciples in these words of the exercises on the Two Standards and Three Kinds of Humility:

> [He charged] . . . them to help all people, first by encouraging them to the highest spiritual poverty, and even to actual poverty if God choose them for it. Secondly, they should encourage them to desire insults and contempt, for from these springs humility . . . and choose poverty with Christ poor, rather than riches; oppression with Christ oppressed, rather than honours . . . I desire to be considered worthless and a fool for Christ, who

suffered such treatment before me, rather than to be thought wise or clever in this world.

(Exx 146, 167)

A community can get an experiential knowledge of true call if it reflects on the pattern of its own sufferings when it has made good decisions and actions. It may be able to recognize that it has experienced the Beatitudes: 'How blessed are the poor in spirit . . . the gentle . . . those who mourn . . . those who hunger and thirst for uprightness . . . the merciful . . . the pure in heart . . . the peacemakers . . . those who are persecuted in the cause of uprightness' (Mt 5:3–12). Community members may find a willingness to be ridiculed for sake of the poor and marginated as they consider certain decisions and actions.

With these gospel values and the advice of Christ in mind the community might consider the ways these values are encouraged and operative in the world beyond the community. It will examine the way forces beyond it encourage the building of a better world. Through social analysis and consideration of the signs of the times it will try to determine the pattern of authentic movements so that it will be able to co-operate with these movements and be instruments of God's grace in our world.

A community might face the call to live a simpler life-style to be in solidarity with the poor. A community might wish to call the poor and marginated into its midst so that it can learn from them. A community might face its own dysfunctional manner of being and realize it is still called to proclaim the good news. It might network with other groups attempting to improve human life on our planet.

Servant

As a community of disciples it will take on the attitudes of Christ as servant to God, to other humans and to the world. 'For the Son of Man himself came not to be served but to serve' (Mk 10:45). If the community is to become a community of disciples in the Lord then it will have to become a serving community of the church and of all humanity. 'Disciple is not superior to teacher' (Mt 10:24). A

140

service orientation will come out of an attitude of love: love for other members of the community, love for all humans, love for various institutions including the church, and love for the earth.

The service of a community of disciples is first to be a witness of the good news. The role of the disciple is to reveal Christ and God's love as it is present in our world, but then to let those it is serving be free and discover the presence of God by themselves. They are to imitate Christ in their relationship to others: 'Yet here am I among you as one who serves!' (Lk 22:27).

I watched a group grow over many years. They were people with high Christian values attempting to live a simple life-style. They supported foster children in their homes, gave themselves in service to the church in roles of leadership, sang in the choir, and participated in the liturgy as lectors and eucharistic ministers. At the same time they promoted a sense of Christian community and consciousness of justice by their life-style and by working for justice in the world.

A new pastor appeared who wished to construct a new church. The group felt that this was an extravagance that the parish could not afford. They also realized that the pastor's reasons had some validity. Even so they went through a discernment process about this issue and how they should act. In the end they mustered reasons against this use of money in the parish and decided to speak up openly in parish meetings with some sense that their reasons might not be accepted.

For about two years they experienced a certain amount of rejection by the pastor and a certain distance from many of their friends in the parish. This was a cause of great suffering and soul-searching among them. They decided to absent themselves from any discussions about building the new church but to continue their participation in the choir, the liturgy and St Vincent de Paul Society activities.

Eventually, they were able to accept the experience of rejection without rancour or publicly criticizing others in the parish. They were given the freedom to suffer for the sake of justice. Then a kind of peaceful reconciliation took place with the pastor and a new respect for the group became present in the parish.

As I write they are not sure whether their objections to a new church will result in a simpler plan or an abandonment of the whole

141

plan. They would like to see the funds for the new church channelled into creative social programmes for abused children but they know now that their ability to accept criticism and rejection as disciples of Christ is a great gift in itself.

Sense of companionship

The communal sense of discipleship demands that the community approach its mission in a spirit of companionship and stewardship. This demands a special kind of humility. Stewards are persons who are responsible for things that they do not own. With all the sense of being favoured and gifted by God, there can be no sense of ownership or élitism in the community. This sense of companionship is to be encouraged in the community in the way it relates to the earth, to its membership, to those beyond the community.

St Paul says, 'People should think of us as Christ's servants, stewards entrusted with the mysteries of God' (1 Co 4:1). So we are to remember that 'It is all one who does the planting and who does the watering, and each will have the proper pay for the work each has done. After all, we do share in God's work' (1 Co 3:9). The universe is free and so are the humans in it. The role of the community is to enhance this freedom. As stewards they will encourage the sense of giftedness among the members, all Christians and all humanity.

APPLICATION TO ACTUAL DECISIONS AND ACTIONS

Seeking spiritual freedom

The community now seeks full spiritual freedom with respect to the particular answer it wishes to discern. It explores the various motivations operating in its being at this time. Members express their state of being as they consider the possible action this answer

142

will entail. They indicate their fears and hopes and describe their initial sense of motivation as they approach the discernment.

Traditionally it is suggested that persons be in a state of grace before making a serious decision for the Lord. This state of grace would include the freedom from sin and disorder and the desire to serve God and God's people. Persons in this state also need to recognize their many motivations at the moment of decision and they need to seek full freedom from them all as they proceed to discern.

A group might well go through some form of reconciliation process among the members and with humanity as a preparation for serious decision. They will pray and seek forgiveness from each other for offences and they will attempt to discover those activities as a group that call for forgiveness from the larger faith community and humanity. Through sharing and penitential rites they will seek forgiveness from each other, from humanity, from the earth and from God.

Communities which have attained these freedoms must also be on the alert lest their decisions and actions are a result of deception under the guise of light. This can easily happen in a group that has achieved peace and trust and is filled with enthusiasm and generosity. Now they need to discern their more subtle motivations and gain a final freedom before making any decision and action.

Freedom and our subtle motivations

Freedom is related to our identity. It is present when we know deeply that we are the beloved of God with all our physical, psychological and spiritual gifts and defects. It gives us self-acceptance in the face of life. It gives us joyful humility. It helps us to face the future with a sense of well-being even though we may be fearful and insecure.

Freedom is usually recognized by our attitude to other persons and to things such as food, shelter and clothing. So, as individuals, we can become aware whether we are free with respect to our health, the goods that we surround ourselves with, or the length of our lives. And as a group we seek freedom regarding our community life with its joys and sorrows.

This sense of freedom also applies to the many psychological motivations that stir in our being. Are we free from the need for approval, the need to be affirmed, the need to be in control, the desire to be at the top in our profession, to be better than others, to have power over others? Depending on our state of being we might say that these needs are not bad in themselves, but they can control us unduly and hinder our openness to the desires of God and our interrelationships with other persons and so we seek freedom in these matters.

Christ suggests that one of the important agents to bring us to freedom is knowledge of the truth: 'The truth will set you free' (Jn 8:32). There are a number of activities that a group might perform to foster such freedom. It must first become aware of the unfreedoms in its own inner relationships. This can be done through interchange among the group or through dialogue with a group guide. This aspect of freedom comes with knowledge. Sometimes the group needs to consider the various psychological forces at play within it. At other times it needs to face the impact of culture and exterior social structures on its life.

Freedom comes with hard work for a conversion is called for – knowledge first, and then a determined effort to gain the freedom wanted, whether it be on a physical, psychological or spiritual level.

A group may gain psychological freedom by exercising itself against certain unfreedoms it may have developed over the years. For example members can determine to be forthright with each other at all times and practise ways of doing this without causing hurt feelings and disintegration of the group. Members can learn to check the interior drives that prove destructive to the group and to others.

Physical and psychological freedoms tend to focus on the immediate relationships within the group. There is a legitimate love that the group should have for itself, but spiritual freedom takes this to another level where the group is confronted by the love of God and the desire of God for itself and for the whole human race. Jesus, who had the fullness of this freedom, becomes the paradigm of this freedom for the group. Spiritual freedom will come with an interpersonal relationship with Christ. The group can go to his

144

example of freedom and pray that the Holy Spirit will share it with us.

Communal decisions in freedom

A group needs to reflect on its freedom in relation to the issue being decided. It may know that even if it wished for certain freedoms the parameters of the group might not allow it to consider them. For example, a group of married men and women with children have to make decisions in terms of these responsibilities.

Time, place, food and rest are usually huge problems for a group. In terms of the issue at hand the group will need to express its limits in these respects and seek to gain the necessary freedom by planning.

Coming to freedom with respect to psychological motivation is more difficult. Much discussion by members about their psychological needs and expectations will be necessary. Each person may have to reflect and share what is happening interiorly as the process proceeds.

The group as group also has its motivations and these are even more subtle. A group guide may be necessary to help a group recognize these and to guide the group to freedom through reflection and sharing.

Spiritual freedom is of ultimate importance when a group desires to be an instrument of God's love and goodness in our world. It involves taking on the mind and heart of Christ as the group proceeds to decision. The members and the group as a whole will pray to be part of the dying and rising of Christ as it proceeds to decision. When they recount their hopes and desires with respect to an issue, they will do this in terms of the ways in which they envision the possible positive and negative outcomes of a decision and action.

This would seem to agree with the kind of freedom St Ignatius looks for in one who is gathering the data for a decision:

I must be indifferent, without any disordered attachment, so that I may not be more inclined or disposed to accept than to give up the object in question. I should be like a balance at equilib-

rium, without leaning to either side, that I might be ready to
follow wherever I feel is more for the glory and praise of God
our Lord and for my salvation.

(Exx 179)

Similarly when considering the advantages and disadvantages that
would accrue to the group from a particular action, each person
knowing his or her identity within the group, can be in touch with
and reckon those spiritual motives that are 'solely for the praise of
God' (Exx 181).

Steps in coming to decision

Certain steps will assist the group in this phase of discernment:
clarifying the issue; developing an open question; gathering possible
answers; choosing a key answer for discernment; composing itself
for discernment; seeking spiritual freedom; praying to the Holy
Spirit for guidance; stating the answer in a positive and negative
way; gathering the spiritual data for all sides of the possible answer;
discerning and choosing the decision; seeking an initial interior
confirmation; beginning the implementation process; seeking further
interior confirmation, and seeking exterior confirmation from a
larger faith community.[5]

Clarifying the issue may take up most of the time in the process.
The members of the community by means of dialogue and discussion attempt to come to agreement on the issue they wish to
deal with.

Once the issue is known the community will state it as an open
question. This means there are a number of possible answers to the
question. A closed question focuses on one answer, e.g., 'Should we
open a drop-in centre in our neighbourhood?' An open question
might be 'What can we do to assist the unemployed in our city?'

Now the community through a kind of brain-storming activity
might seek answers to the open question. Through dialogue and
discussion it chooses one answer to deal with first. It will state its
answer positively and negatively, for example, 'We will support a
refugee family.' 'We will not support a refugee family.'

Once the possible answer has been determined each member of

the group privately develops a list of advantages and disadvantages for the positive and negative expression of the statement. These four lists are then shared with the total group so that each member has a composite of reasons for or against both the positive and negative expressions of the statement.

Each person prays with the composite four lists of reasons and makes a provisional decision. After this the group shares the results of prayer indicating their individual decisions along with the main reasons for and against. If unanimity is not reached the group discusses the main reasons for and against the answer and through this process can reach a consensus that both satisfies and challenges each member of the group.

The grace desired

As the group seeks to decide its best course of action in terms of God's desire it composes itself to respond freely to the initiative of God. It may recall these words: 'Look, I am standing at the door, knocking. If one of you hears me calling and opens the door, I will come in to share a meal at that person's side' (Rv 3:20).

A further element in composing the community is its immediate relationship to God. It enters the remainder of the discernment in a sense of humility and need. It wishes to be fully open, fully available to God as a community of disciples. It will recall its foundational hopes and desires and its images of itself as a community of disciples. It offers all its discussions, pains, prayers and itself to God as it proceeds with the discernment.

Discerning the dominant spiritual reasons for choosing

Advantages and disadvantages may be experienced with or without any feeling component. In a state of freedom they are to be judged as good or better reasons. We come to decision 'in the matter proposed because of weightier movement of my (our) reason, not because of any sensual attractions' (Exx 182).

In the process of finding, reflecting and sharing the weightier spiritual motivations the group may come to freedom; if not, it is doubtful if the decision is being properly discerned. The spiritual reasons refer to those opportunities that the group considers will help or hinder it in its vocation to work with Christ for the betterment of humanity. When the community is trying to assemble the spiritual advantages and disadvantages of the positive and negative statements of the possible action, it may help it to list all of the material and psychological advantages and disadvantages as well, for they can surface spiritual data that may have been neglected. But the spiritual significance of the advantages and disadvantages becomes dominant in determining the choice.

Decision

After reporting the results of prayer over the composite of four lists of reasons the group should discuss the spiritual motivations that moved them.

The examples of Christ's teachings and his service to humanity bring forth the values the community follows in making its choice. The group will also consider the ways its relationship with the person of Christ will be enhanced or diminished by doing or not doing the action under consideration. Sometimes this will mean the willingness and even desire to suffer with Christ for the cause of justice. At other times it will mean the acceptance of joy and fulfilment in being instruments of Christ's goodness and love to others.

At this time the community might recall the patterns of deception and true call it has recognized in reflecting on its graced history. It will remember examples such as communities like L'Arche and the environmental movement which call it to truth and those such as racism and profiteering which deceive and turn it in on itself. This awareness will assist it in finding consensus and in seeking confirmation.

Confirmation

Time should be given for an experience of confirmation from the Lord. This is to assure the group that their desires fit in with the desires of God. Otherwise they might be in the position of those people who make decisions and then call upon God to approve them and bring them to successful conclusions (cf. Exx 154). The group seeks an interior confirmation from its own prayer and an exterior confirmation from a larger faith community.

The spiritual consolation of confirmation has a past, present and future element in it. The group senses that its decision and action will be a continuation of its light-filled history and in congruity with its vision, dreams, hopes and desires. The group has a sense of union with Christ even as it faces the difficulties the action will entail. Conviction is present in the group. Along with conviction there is peace, joy and energy to move into the future with Christ.

Exercises: discerning movement of spirits in a community

A group that wishes to be an apostolic community will need to distinguish those movements of spirits that call it to truth from those which call it into falsehood. Two exercises may assist a group in such discernment. Each exercise has three steps:

1. Private reflection on the group's communal experience.
2. Group focusing and sharing on specific experiences.
3. Further reflection and sharing, closing with prayer.

The first exercise uses theological reflection or consideration of the signs of the times to analyse the group's situation *vis-à-vis* its present context. The second builds on the communal history of the group.

EXERCISE XI: DISCERNING THE 'GOOD AND BAD ANGELS' IN GROUP DECISION-MAKING

PRIVATE REFLECTION

Contextualizing

If a cause precedes, consolation can come from either the good spirit (angel) or the evil one, but for quite different purposes. The good spirit (angel) consoles so that the soul may make progress and advance from what is good to what is better. The evil one consoles for purposes that are the contrary, and so that afterwards it might draw the soul to its own perverse intentions and towards evil. (Exx 331)

Imaging

We image ourselves with the disciples listening to Jesus as he explains the activities of the good and evil angels.

The grace desired

We seek from the Lord a knowledge of deceptions in our communal life and help to guard against them and a knowledge of the true ways the Lord calls our community and help to respond to them in our role as disciples of Christ.

Pointing

Consider some 'good angels' (outside forces) we have experienced in our community life and decision-making from societal and religious sources.

Consider some 'bad angels' (outside forces) we have experienced in our community life and decision-making from societal and religious sources.

Colloquy

Thank the Lord for what happened to me in prayer and I ask God to help me present my experience to the group. The *Lord's Prayer*.

GROUP SHARING

The group focuses on and shares specific experiences:

Name these and focus on those where all members of the community were present.

Describe the movements in each instance:
- What was the context of the experience?
- What was the group considering?
- What took place in the group?
- How did it turn out?

How would you discern these forces with your group in the future?

FURTHER SHARING FROM THE PREVIOUS REFLECTION

- What did I hear?
- What impressed me as the others shared?
- What new insights did I gain?
- What are the inevitable consequences of the truths we have shared?
- Where did I experience affective harmony with the others as they spoke about discernment?

Group colloquy

We speak to the Lord about the insights we have gained and we ask the Lord to choose us to follow him under the standard of his cross. The *Lord's Prayer*.

EXERCISE XII: DISCERNING PATTERNS OF DECEPTION AND OF TRUE CALL

PRIVATE REFLECTION

Context

'You are the Christ, the Son of the living God.' . . . 'Simon son of Jonah, you are a blessed man!' . . . Jesus began to make it clear to his disciples that he was destined to go to Jerusalem and suffer grievously . . . 'Heaven preserve you, Lord,' he said, 'this must not happen to you.' . . . 'Get behind me, Satan! You are an obstacle in my path, because you are thinking not as God thinks but as human beings do.' . . . If any want to become followers of mine, let them renounce themselves and take up their cross and follow me.' (cf. Mt 16:13–26)

Imaging

We image ourselves with the disciples listening to this interchange between Jesus and Peter.

The grace desired

I seek from the Lord a knowledge of deceptions in our communal life and help to guard against them and a knowledge of the true ways the Lord calls our community and help to respond to them in our role as disciples of Christ.

Pointing

Deceptions come in the form of light or goodness. To discover the pattern of deception in one's life it is wise to know one's virtuous tendencies and one's gifts of light and goodness and then check out the exaggeration of these virtues and gifts.

- What virtues and gifts, in all humility, do I sense in our community?
- How do I see these being exaggerated?
- What patterns of deception do I recognize in our community?

True calls from the Lord often come in unexpected ways and are

152

often as paradoxical as the beatitudes. To discover the pattern of true calls in our life it is helpful to look at the beginning concerns, fears and weaknesses that our deepest desires stir up in us and to follow these movements through to the complete sense of call.

- How do I sense we as a community have been drawn beyond ourselves towards Christ in the past?
- Where have we felt insecurity and fear of commitment along with desire to be and work with the Lord?
- How does this compare with the suggestions of Ignatius: 'Encourage them to the highest spiritual poverty, humiliations and humility', and the desire 'to be poor with Christ poor . . . and to be insulted with Christ insulted' (Exx 146)?
- What pattern of call do I recognize in our community?

Colloquy

I thank the Lord for what happened to me in prayer and I ask God to help me present my experience to the group. The *Lord's Prayer*.

GROUP SHARING

The group shares the results of private reflection paying special attention to the patterns of deception and call that they recognize in the group.

FURTHER SHARING FROM THE PREVIOUS REFLECTION

- What did I hear?
- What impressed me as the others shared?
- What new insights did I gain?
- What are the inevitable consequences of the truths we have shared?
  - Where did I experience affective harmony with the others as they spoke about discernment?

Group colloquy

We speak to the Lord about the insights we have gained and we ask the Lord to choose us to follow him under the standard of his cross. The *Lord's Prayer*.

NOTES

[1] *The Freedom of God and the God of Freedom* (The Hibbert Trust, London, 1985), p. 6.

[2] Cf. Karl Rahner SJ: *The Dynamic Element in the Church* (Palm Publishers, Montreal, 1964), pp. 110–114, and Jerome Murphy-O'Connor OP: *Becoming Human Together* (Michael Glazier Inc., Wilmington, Delaware, 1982), pp. 118–9.

[3] 'Power is the free commitment of individuals to articulated goals and objectives that they have freely chosen' *ISECP* manual, volume 1, p. 37.

[4] Deceptive patterns lead to an unauthentic life. For the philosopher Bernard Lonergan SJ, unauthenticity ensues when persons fail to follow a dynamic of being attentive, being intelligent, being reasonable and being responsible. Authenticity is achieved in self-transcendence. This takes place when persons experience the love of God flooding their hearts and are moved to live a life in love with God. To live an authentic life Lonergan suggests persons fulfil the transcendental precepts: be attentive, be intelligent, be reasonable, be responsible and be in love. See *Method in Theology* (Herder and Herder, New York, 1972), pp. 103–9.

[5] These steps were developed by Remi Limoges SJ in collaboration with Susan Breckel RSM, Margaret Brennan IHM and myself for ten-day 'Discernment and Christian Governance Workshops' we presented between 1976 and 1986.

CONFIRMATION

Then they said to each other, 'Did not our hearts burn within us as he talked to us on the road and explained the scriptures to us?' They set out that instant and returned to Jerusalem. There they found the Eleven assembled together with their companions, who said to them, 'The Lord has indeed risen and has appeared to Simon.' Then they told their story of what had happened to them on the road and how they had recognized him at the breaking of bread.

(Lk 24:32–5)

Convinced and energized as a community might be after reaching a discerned decision in consensus there is still one further activity to perform in the decision part of the process. This is to ask the Lord to give a sense of confirmation. What this demands of the group is another level of spiritual freedom, a freedom that is not only a condition for proceeding with the process but also a sign of consolation.

When a group comes to this moment in its discernment it returns to the insights and awareness that preceded its decision – its desire to go beyond communal self-centredness, its sense of intimacy with Christ, and its awareness of authentic and deceptive calls. It recalls the steps it took as it moved to express its call in a concrete decision. Now is the moment when the full significance of Ignatius' principle that 'good decisions are made in the time of spiritual consolation' (Exx 318) is most operative. An experience of confirmation is in itself a spiritual consolation. Once again the group needs to discern its interior movement of spirits.

The dominant experience of confirmation in the group is union of minds and hearts, but in conjunction with the experience Ignatius describes as consolation: 'increase of faith, hope and love . . . joy and peace' (Exx 316). So let us focus on the communal processes of discerning experiences of confirmation.

The group will deal with many experiences from within itself and from beyond itself that can be hopeful or fearful, painful or enjoyable. It will become more conscious of those dimensions in its life and activity that are dying and those that are rising. Maturity comes as the group is able to recognize and accept these experiences as a continuation of the sufferings and joys of Jesus Christ.

The group experiences the paschal mystery most fully as it prays for confirmation. Experiences of dying and rising are grist for an awareness that the decision is being confirmed by God. Both are expressions of spiritual consolation. The group places itself at the foot of the cross as well as in the upper room as it seeks from the Lord a sense of confirmation with its decision.

The group which described its life experience under the image of an unwanted step-child (page 46) eventually discerned that they should separate from the larger group and go it alone. As they prayed over this decision they were quite frightened. They realized that much of their past history was based on an interchange with the larger group in which they were constantly fighting for recognition.

They also recalled the meaning they had found in their history, summing it up with the scripture passage: 'The stone that the builders rejected has become the cornerstone' (Lk 20:17). They recognized and accepted themselves as part of the paschal mystery of the body of Christ.

As the group anticipated the pain and cost of its decision it was given the willingness to continue to suffer as a step-child might. In poverty and humility it experienced the consolation of insight and energy. They were able to say with Paul: 'It makes me happy to be suffering for you now, and in my own body to make up all the hardships that still have to be undergone by Christ for the sake of his body, the church' (Col 1:24).

Experiences of discipleship

What makes these experiences consolation is the sense of being with Jesus Christ in his suffering and glory. The disciple not only desires to take on the mind and heart of Christ but desires to experience what Jesus Christ experienced, albeit in a different historical con-

156

text. In their desire to share in both the sufferings and the glories of Jesus Christ disciples recognize that the costs as well as the joys of discipleship can be experiences of consolation.

Ignatius warns us that it is necessary to be on one's guard to recognize the serpent's tail in an exaggerated desire for suffering and glory or in attributing all suffering and glory to the action of the Holy Spirit.There are examples of religious fanaticism in which suffering and martyrdom rather than the betterment of humanity are the be-all and end-all of the action. True humility is both a requisite and an experience of discernment. Often when a group has come to decision by consensus there is such relief that they wish to proceed immediately into action. Yet psychologically and spiritually this is not a good move. An extreme exuberance and feeling of achievement without realism may in fact be an experience of desolation. A certain inflated corporate ego can exist: 'We're ahead of others in this field. We'll really lead the pack', or similar thoughts can be present. They indicate an unrealistic sense of achievement.

Two other attitudes can also express desolation. There can be an over-optimism that 'God will provide', which is really an attempt to escape from the planning that is needed. The group is unwilling to face the difficulties of implementing the decision. It does not know the strategy for planning or it does not know how to redirect its energy as it faces anticipated obstacles. This desolation flows from an unwillingness to accept our responsibility for building a better world. The group is overwhelmed with attempting to har-monize all the variables of history and God's overall design for humanity. It has forgotten the Ignatian maxim: 'Pray and so work as if it all depends on us. Leave the success of the venture to God.'

The second experience of desolation tends to flow from a pessi-mistic frame of mind. The group is overwhelmed by the anticipated difficulties and becomes discouraged. It tends to give up and even deny the rightness of the original decision. Or the group might make half-hearted efforts at implementation, but with unrealistic time lines, with little communication among themselves and beyond themselves, poor delegation, and a lack of support for those implementing the decision.

Such desolations need to be faced or the group will not recall its desire to be an instrument of God's love for humanity even in the face of suffering and difficulties. It will not focus on its God-given talents. It will not rely on the gifts of the Holy Spirit to assist it in implementing its decision. Ignatius suggests that there can come a time when all we have is our faith in God's merciful and creative grace to help us overcome such desolation.

Occasions for experiencing confirmation

There are three moments of confirmation of a decision: the first is during the decision-making itself, the second occurs when the group is involved in implementation issues, and the third occurs as the action proceeds. The group will recognize the consolation of confirmation by discerning the significance of the movement of spirits within its interchange as it moves through these three moments.

St Ignatius felt that the commitment demanded by a possible decision should be faced during the time of decision. In the *Spiritual Exercises* he deals with this in terms of intimacy with Jesus. After about twenty prayer periods seeking an 'intimate knowledge of our Lord made human for me', Ignatius suggests that there are three kinds of love for God and that the person making a decision seek the third kind. The person prays for deep union with Christ, desiring and choosing 'poverty with Christ poor . . . oppression with Christ oppressed . . . to be considered worthless and a fool for Christ' (Exx 167). For Ignatius suffering with Christ was a privilege. We were to respond as St Peter and St John did in Jerusalem: 'They rejoiced that they were considered worthy to suffer dishonour for the sake of the name' (Acts 5:41). When a community realizes that this special kind of intimacy with Jesus Christ is possible if it carries out its particular decision, it should see it as a special sign of God's approval – confirmation – for its enterprise with Jesus Christ.

Another moment of confirmation may come as the community attends to the elements of implementation, for then members fully realize the work entailed in bringing the decision into act. At this time the community has to make a series of practical decisions on time line, budgeting of resources and delegating of responsibilities. It will still be looking for further indications that its decision is confirmed. Realistically facing these costs in terms of hoped-for results in building the realm of God may strengthen the resolve of the group. They may actually gain new energy to carry out the decision. Realistic resolve and further energy are signs of confirmation.

As the action proceeds a community will look for a sense of being confirmed in itself rather than for some outside sign that its decision is correct and approved by God. It will recognize that it is having a new sense of unity, a new sense of humility, a new sense of well-being. It will realize that it is being energized and called beyond itself as an instrument of God's love in our world. It will know itself differently. It will recognize a sense of being in and with Christ as it proceeds to put its decision into action.

As we have seen, the desire to be with Christ in the sufferings and joys that a decision may bring forth is a consolation and a sign that the dispositions of a group are good. If the group faces the possible sufferings that a decision may entail with equanimity and even with desire, this is an experience of the consolation of confirmation. However, even when a community is experiencing suffering or joy during the implementation of the decision the interior state of the group still has to be discerned to know if this is the consolation of confirmation. Both interior and exterior experiences of suffering and joy, success and failure, have to be discerned.

When a group uses a discernment process for decision and action it naturally looks for exterior signs of confirmation. These are usually the fulfilment of objectives and goals that the group wished when it began the process. But once again the exterior signs of confirmation require discernment. As the group discerns and appropriates this exterior confirmation it returns to the interior life of its members and itself, although it may be that the interpretation of a confirmed call to this or that application will be determined by someone else or by later circumstances.

There is an example in the *Autobiography* of St Ignatius. Ignatius and his early companions felt that they were to go on pilgrimage to Jerusalem. But a war between Venice and the Turks prevented this. After waiting for a number of months for a ship to Jerusalem these men went to Rome to minister to the people and to see the Pope. Upon hearing their desires it was Pope Julius III who said to them, 'Rome is your Jerusalem.' The story of St Francis Regis also illustrates this. Francis Regis felt called by God to work in the Canadian missions along with John Brebeuf and his companions. His provincial acknowledged the call, but asked him to experience these hardships among the poor mountain people of Southern France.

A sign of interior confirmation of a decision is a group's freedom to adjust to various outside forces. The group continues to discern and so can recognize that the objective confirmation of its decision may be somewhat different from what it expected. Yet this objective confirmation is not opposed to its basic decision.

The sense of being missioned

The experience of confirmation as a group moves into the future in terms of being called forth in Christ is usually a sense of being missioned. The full sense of mission is subjective and requires discernment, although the group may experience an objective sign of mission such as encouragement from persons outside the group or from an experience of success.

A sense of a group's mission and an experience of confirmation go hand-in-hand. The group will operate from a sense of mission before and during a decision-making process and return to its sense of mission when seeking confirmation. It will probably experience a further sense of mission when it is given an experience of confirmation of the decision.

The sense of mission is given to it in two different ways. One is like a push from within the group as it considers its own vision and goals, desires and energies, identity and vocation. The other is like a pull from beyond the group, a call or challenge from the church or humanity.

A group's mission will usually be expressed by certain specific activities. Yet mission is more than these. It is a style of being present to the world as disciples of Christ.[1] It is also a way of proceeding. The activity of using communal discernment to come to decisions and go into action is in itself an expression of mission.

Using the process we have been suggesting, a group will have arrived at clarity regarding its specific mission by going through its life cycle. This leads it through a process of sharing its vision, dreams, desires and hopes, and developing its goals and objectives before moving to a definitive decision. As it seeks confirmation the group will again be in touch with this movement of the life cycle. It will test its decision against this movement. An element in the experience of confirmation will be a sense of congruence between its decision and its mission. This sense of congruence will indicate to the group that its decision will fulfil its basic mission.

An example of confirmation

Sometimes the experience of confirmation is only known when one member reveals his or her pain to a group. The consolation is experienced as a sense of the suffering Christ in the group at the time of decision. I know a group that experienced the pain of two of its members in the process of separation and divorce.

The married couple announced to the group that they were considering separation and divorce. The rest of the group was quite confused and deeply felt their pain. They feared for the breakup of the group. What were they to do? They realized that they were being called to a new freedom. They had to be free enough to let the community die. After much prayer and discussion the group was given this kind of freedom.

They also realized that they had to re-image the community if these persons were to stay with it. They sensed they were being called to support the couple and their children in this painful experience. Yet all the group could do was be with each member of the family and support them individually.

In the following meetings much suffering was experienced. At first the couple was not able to reveal the reasons for the state of affairs. Gradually in this free and non-judgemental atmosphere they and their children were able to open up and express their interior selves to the group.

A deeper experience of community came about. Deep spiritual needs and experiences were disclosed and the total group changed as the sharing proceeded. Everyone knew that supporting the family in pain had brought forth something new. They experienced renewed freedom, love and respect with each other, and a new identity. The group was able to recognize the suffering of Christ taking place in the group. With this realization, conviction came that the group could truly witness to a new expression of faith community in our world. Its existence and sense of mission were confirmed.

Discerning confirmation

Sometimes a community will know, at the time of decision, from its inner relationships and sense of itself that its decision is confirmed by an experience similar to that of its unique communal spiritual consolation. However, a community usually has to investigate its process once it has reached a decision. The satisfaction that it has not skimped on proper process will often initiate the consolation of confirmation. This investigation will involve looking back through a number of activities that ensure that its unique history as well as its sense of call and giftedness from God are activated. It will examine whether it had a sense of freedom and spiritual consolation during the steps of decision-making.

Returning to its history it may ask: 'Did we pray with our communal graced history and create our history line?' 'Did we reflect and share our unique sense of communal spiritual consolation?'

Reflecting on its membership it may ask: 'Did we appreciate and use the various gifts of the persons in our community?'[2] 'Did we share the gifts of our contemplations on the life of Christ and the disciples?'

It may ask: 'As we decided, did we consider our basic call to be instruments of God's truth, goodness and love in our world?' 'Did we face the various forces influencing us from within our community and from beyond it?' 'As we came to the decision phase of discernment did we follow good process?' 'Were we open and peaceful during this part? Was there an initial sense of spiritual consolation as we decided?'

Similar concerns about the sense of spiritual consolation arise as the group recalls the steps it followed in the fifth phase of discernment, the decision and action phase (chapter 8). 'Did we follow the steps faithfully?' 'Were we open and peaceful during this part?' 'Was there an initial sense of spiritual consolation as we decided?'

The experience of confirmation: summary

How would a faith community of today describe the experience of the consolation of confirmation? Among other elements the community will have a sense of freedom, realism and peace along with joy and energy for the task.

In the experience of confirmation a realism will be present. The cost in carrying out the action will be recognized. They might even consider the obstacles to be overcome as an occasion for fulfilling the decision or at least as an opportunity to suffer with Christ (and the whole of humanity). The community will experience the joy of discipleship. A sense of joy in the anticipated sufferings and burden of the work may be experienced.

And with this there are hope and energy, not only for the individual members of the community, nor just for the community itself, but for all humanity. The hope and energy draw members forth to be instruments of God's grace for our world. 'The love of Christ urges' (2 Co 5:14) them on for the betterment of humanity, moving the group to consider unjust sinful structures that they might develop grace-filled structures first among themselves and then beyond themselves. A sign of the consolation of confirmation will be the community's appreciation of the freedom of all humans before God and a willingness to admit plurality of cultures, religions and spiritualities as the human race tries to achieve unity.

Experiences of struggle and lack of conviction may occur within the community as people consider the cost of discipleship, yet the community is carried beyond itself even to bring gospel values to the whole human race. Of course, such suffering and joy have to be examined lest the group turn in on itself in self-righteousness and extreme criticism of 'the world'.

The basic experience of the consolation of confirmation is a sense of unity with each other and a sense of fellowship in and with the Lord. This should be present when a group reaches a decision and when it is seeking confirmation. Felt experiences of unity and fellowship are signs of the consolation of confirmation.

Consensus in communal decision-making

The consolation of consensus in a group is a special form of confirmation. As a group moves to final decision it looks for full agreement or union, a sense of consensus. A group might say that a majority vote gives a consensus. This would mean that every member in the group is committed to the decision so reached by this majority vote. Such agreement may be enough for a united commitment to action. Others may say that only unanimity is the experience of consensus that expresses full agreement and union. I believe that consensus means more than either of these; only after a group dynamic in which everyone has fully participated can such agreement and union be termed consensus. While majority rule works in parliamentary procedure, discerning faith communities usually hope for unanimity in their decisions.

Sometimes a spokesperson for the group is able to express this union very well. The Quakers after much discussion over a proposition look to a respected member of the meeting (its clerk) to express the sense of the meeting. If the clerk is gifted with discernment the meeting will express unanimity in the clerk's sense of the meeting, and can then move into implementation.

The Quakers believe that the spirit of the group will bring forth an expression of consensus if the group is open and practises much patience. Unanimity is not present when a number of the members do not have a sense of individual consolation about a decision. A group whose members are honest with each other and who have a deep desire for the reign of God can find a unanimous consensus within itself. The group has a deep sense that this is a true experience of unanimity and not a manipulated one. This will be affirmed by an experience of spiritual consolation.[3]

When unanimity is not present the group should begin a process to discover where unanimity lies. The differences may be such that a group will have to pray over them in terms of its basic vision and goals to see if another expression of the proposal can be made and unanimity discovered. When the number of dissenting voices over a proposition is small it is important that the group listen carefully to the reasons against the proposition. Sometimes these are matters of implementation and if proper conditions are expressed in the proposition the group can come to unanimity. It is still very important for the group to deal with the items over which members struggled. Some of the disadvantages members found, for example, will be significant in implementing the decision. These might be pitfalls to be avoided and cautions to be taken.

Acknowledging the differences in the group and trying to use the disadvantages as instruments for better implementation often bring the group to a sense of peace and union. It is still important that the group seek the consolation of confirmation of its unanimous decision.

The fruits of consensus

The group I referred to as the unwanted step-child followed the many steps mentioned above. As they came to the time of decision and implementation they recalled their consolation of insight into their own experience of the paschal mystery and the willingness to consider suffering with the body of Christ in the future. As they prayed for confirmation on their decision they realized as a group that the decision might well lead them into experiences similar to the step-child ones they had found in their communal graced history. But now they faced this in a mature way with equanimity and willingness to face such pain in the future for the sake of the body of Christ.

The experience of union in conjunction with faith, hope, love, peace and joy is the experience of the consolation of consensus. The group may realize that suffering will be involved in implementation. Yet the group is united and may even experience a special sense of its wholeness.

Everyone in the group will be satisfied that they and the others have been listened to, that the gifts of each member have been acknowledged. Everyone will be at rest with the outcome of the process, sensing that a free and effective process has been followed. Everyone will be committed to the decision and its implementation.

The group will know itself as beloved of God. It recognizes this love actually working in the group. It will see how this love frees everyone so that creative gifts get expressed; the creative action of the group as a whole takes place before its eyes. This may surprise the group and release a sense of wonder.

The group has a sense of being energized and drawn into the future in spite of its limitations. It relates to its own past sufferings in working toward achieving the reign of God and willingly anticipates similar sufferings in the future. It enters the effort of implementing the decision with a realistic hope and a certain joy in the power of the risen Christ. The group can make Paul's prayer its own: '. . . that I may come to know Christ and the power of his resurrection, and partake of his sufferings . . .' (Ph 3:10).

Part of the experience of consensus will include the sense that carrying out a decision will be an expression of 'finding God in all things that we may better love and serve God in all things'.

The consolation will be experienced as gift. One or many of the gifts of the Holy Spirit will be recognized as a special sense of giftedness coming from beyond the group. It may experience a creativity it didn't know it had, hope in the face of obstacles, or a sense of universal compassion. When it reflects on these experiences it may have an awareness of transcendence. It may sense that its unity is in that of the Godhead, that its sense of beautiful persons is in the beauty of God, its sense of rightness is in the truth that is God, its sense of goodness is in the goodness of God, and its knowledge of its human gifts is of an extension of Jesus Christ.

NEW TESTAMENT EXPERIENCES OF CONFIRMATION

A community can learn much from New Testament experiences of communal confirmation, such as are found in the mission and return of the disciples to Jerusalem (Luke 10), the action of the two disciples at Emmaus (Luke 24), the religious experience on Pentecost (Acts 2), the suffering of Peter and John (Acts 5), the council

166

at Jerusalem (Acts 15), and the many descriptions of courageous decisions under persecution of the small churches founded by Paul.

Gospels

After the disciples report to Jesus about the success of their mission Jesus warns them about over-exuberance at their new-found power. Then while rejoicing with them he realizes that the Father has confirmed them in their mission and exclaims: 'I bless you, Father, Lord of heaven and of earth, for hiding these things from the learned and the clever and revealing them to little children: yes, Father, for that is what it has pleased you to do' (Lk 10:21).

As a result of their encounter with Christ on the road to Emmaus, the disciples said,

> 'Did not our hearts burn within us as he talked to us on the road, and explained the scriptures to us?' They set out that instant and returned to Jerusalem. There they found the Eleven assembled together with their companions, who said to them, 'The Lord has indeed risen, and has appeared to Simon.' Then they told their story of what had happened on the road and how they had recognized him at the breaking of bread.
>
> (Lk 24:32–5)

These disciples had two experiences of consolation: their hearts burning as Christ explained the scriptures to them and then recognizing him at the breaking of bread. These consolations energized them to return and tell the good news to their friends. Then they experienced a confirmation of their decision to return to Jerusalem by the witness of the other disciples to the resurrection.

Acts

At Pentecost, the early faith community experiences being carried right into mission by the inspiration of the Holy Spirit. As described in Acts this experience in the early church is a communal consolation that cannot be doubted. As such it carries with it its own

167

confirmation. The interior changes in the disciples from fearful persons to bold people, from stammering persons to eloquent persons, indicate the power of the experience. The exterior results of the disciples preaching and their audience's response also confirm the self-evidence of the experience: 'Parthians, Medes . . . Cretans and Arabs; we hear them preaching in our own language about the marvels of God' (Ac 2:9–11). Ignatius classified this kind of experience as a consolation without previous cause, saying that 'there can be no deception in it, since it can come only from God our Lord' (Exx 336).

After their imprisonment and sufferings, Peter and John are given a joyful awareness 'that they have had the honour of suffering humiliation for the sake of the name' (Ac 5:41). They recognize a certain objective confirmation in the fact of their sufferings, for proclaiming the good news of Jesus Christ is a sign of union with Christ in his suffering and death. The desire for such suffering then becomes a criterion for testing further decisions and actions.

The Council of Jerusalem is an excellent example of the way the process worked in the early church. The church had an experience. This experience brought about a crisis. The council faced the implications of gentile baptism. It listened to the experiences of its members. It discussed very thoroughly the implications of possible decisions in a state of conflict and with heated debate. It prayed over all this and arrived at a decision. It realized this was confirmed by the Holy Spirit. It determined how to communicate its decision. In doing this it indicated to the church at large the process it had followed, its decision regarding the gentiles' baptismal obligations, and its sense of confirmation: 'It has been decided by the Holy Spirit and by us ourselves' (Ac 15:28).

St Paul

In the letters of St Paul to the early Christian communities we find many expressions of confirmation. These may be the best source of insight into confirmation in a community. Paul is able to confirm the church of Thessalonika in its sufferings: ' . . . that you may be found worthy of the kingdom of God; it is for the sake of this that you are suffering now' (2 Th 1:5). He points out to the church of Colossae how God is working in them in 'the love that you show towards all God's holy people' (Col 1:4).

With the risen Christ as head and his body the believing community there is a unity of person. The risen Christ is the mind and heart of the body. This unity is more than a moral unity that brings about co-ordination and co-operation for a unified action. It is a coexisting unity (cf. 1 Co 10:17; Rm 12:5, 15). The unity is constantly creative because it lets the members be. In 1 Co 11:23–6 Paul speaks of receiving from the Lord as distinct from doing the eucharistic action that expresses the body of Christ in the world. This is also expressed in Ep 4:11–16 and in Col 2:19: ' . . . by which the whole body, given all that it needs and held together by its joints and sinews, grows with the growth given by God'. It is within the love of Christ that the community has a sense of the One, the Beautiful, the True and the Good (cf. Col 3:14,15).

What we see in the scripture accounts is a realism about life. The early Christians remembered the great sufferings of Christ for them and for the whole human race. They experienced joy in the suffering. They recognized this joy as a grace of union with Christ in his sufferings. They knew that the decisions they were making for the sake of Christ and the gospel would bring opposition. They faced the possibility of suffering and even death in the carrying out of their decisions. They accepted the struggle that is necessary for unity in diversity. They were able to re-express their hope to accommodate various life-styles in the church provided the basic belief that 'Jesus Christ has come in human nature' (1 Jn 4:2) and 'was raised to life for our justification' (Rm 4:25) was sustained.

COMMUNAL SPIRITUAL CONSOLATION AND VARIOUS GROUP DYNAMICS

A number of instruments are helpful for a Christian group when it is discerning decisions in terms of communal spiritual consolation and the experience of confirmation. Good group dynamics in a faith context can be the occasion for the experience of spiritual communal consolation and the experience of spiritual communal consolation is a criterion for judging how the group dynamic is proceeding.

1. Life Cycle

The Life Cycle suggests that the community return to the affective experiences of its initial desire to discern whether the group is experiencing that kind of consolation now. It can return to its growth from its beginnings through its development as a community. This helps the community to check out its decision in terms of its myth. It can then move on to consider the way the community has developed its vision, dream, desires and hopes throughout its history, so the community can ask itself whether it senses continuity and congruity with the graced meaning of its history. If this is felt it is a good indication of the consolation of confirmation.

In the discerning process it is the appropriation of past experiences of intimate knowledge of God's relationship with the group that assists it to recognize an experience of consolation as it is making decisions. Upon reflection the group will realize that its past experiences of spiritual confirmation have entailed a sense of union with Jesus Christ in the paschal mystery.

2. Myers-Briggs Type Indicator

The Myers-Briggs Type Indicator (cf. chapter 5, p. 88 and note) assists people to understand some of their own behaviour and that of others. It is a good instrument for groups because it helps members to be tolerant and to acknowledge the various contributions of others who approach life differently. The different gifts in the group can be called to the fore and communal decisions will be more complete.

When a group is making a decision one process that it might follow is to deal with an issue in terms of its MBTI functions. The group would begin focusing on the Sensate mode then move to the Intuitive mode, then to the Thinking mode and finally to the Feeling mode in its discussion.[4] This process (SNTF) can also be used in checking out a decision made. And if the steps have been followed to the satisfaction of all, the group has enjoyed freedom in its process. Freedom is a necessary preliminary of confirmation.

3. Energy Cycle

The Energy Cycle follows a circular dynamic for reflecting on possible future action with reference to past action. Its phases are: Action →Evaluation→Recommendation→Decision→Action. In this cycle the community starts with an action that came from a previous decision. It evaluates that action and then makes recommendations. Then it proceeds to a new decision. The process helps the group to keep experiencing the kind of spiritual energy it has discovered in its discernment method.

At the time when confirmation is sought the heightened awareness of its communal spiritual consolation gained through the many activities suggested up to now becomes the criterion for checking the Energy Cycle. If the community realizes that it has followed the Energy Cycle to everyone's satisfaction it will experience the consolation of unity and well-being.

In a Christian setting Christian values and perspectives become the criteria for evaluating the action and making recommendations. The question of what spiritual consolations and desolations are moving the group becomes the significant instrument for deciding on a recommendation of the group and executing a decision.

As an action is evaluated the community considers the way it went about implementing its decision. It may ask, 'In the tentative time between decision and confirmation, what quality of presence existed as we decided on items of delegation, communication, finances and operating procedures to ensure the effectiveness of the action?' 'Were we really listening to each other?' 'Did we have a sense of God being with us even though we anticipated the cost of our decision?' 'Was there a willingness to be with Christ in suffering as well as joy?'

A group might consider three sets of criteria. The first would be somewhat material, e.g., 'Did we make the necessary profit we looked for?' The second would be concerned with values, e.g., 'Did the action promote Christian values?' A third set, concerned with spiritual consolation while the action is taking place, is important at confirmation time: 'Did God give us an in-depth awareness that we were instruments in building the realm of God as the action happened?' 'Was there a sense of deeper Christian love among us and those involved than before the action?' 'Were we in spiritual consolation as we evaluated our previous action?' The group will also question whether it senses that the action fulfilled the deeper affective relationship with Christ that its vision and charism desire.

EXERCISE XIII: MAKING THE DECISION AND SEEKING CONFIRMATION[5]

This exercise has two parts: making the decision and seeking confirmation. The group process in both parts assists the group to discern what it is to do and energizes it for action. After the group has come to a decision, it is recommended that some time be allowed for an experience of confirmation.

A. Making the decision

Contextualizing

It is my prayer that your love for one another may grow more and more with the knowledge and complete understanding that will help you to come to true discernment. (Ph 1:9–10)

Imaging

We imagine ourselves within the group holding the results of our personal prayer as a gift in our hands.

The grace desired

We ask the Lord to help us be attentive to the results of the prayer of each member and help us discern the will of God from this data.

172

Pointing

The group uses the following process to come to decision:

In the group each member states his or her provisional decision.

Each member in turn then states the reason which had the most weight in his or her decision.

After a brief period of silent reflection members share their feelings about having (or not having) reached a decision.

If a decision was not reached, the group will then have to discover through dialogue where consensus actually exists in the matter under consideration. In the light of this consensus the group may proceed with the decision with certain implementing provisos or, if necessary, refocus the question, formulate other answers, or consider some of the alternative answers previously formulated.

Group colloquy

Coming before the Lord, the group expresses its belief in God's goodness and presence and its hope for the future in terms of reaching or not reaching a decision at this time. The *Lord's Prayer*.

B. The experience of confirmation

When a decision is reached with the consensus of the group it may then have time to perform the following exercise of seeking confirmation.

PRIVATE REFLECTION

Contextualizing

Blessed be the God and Father of our Lord Jesus Christ, the merciful Father and the God who gives every possible encouragement; God supports us in every hardship, so that we are able to come to the support of others in every hardship of theirs because of the encouragement that we ourselves receive from God. For just as the sufferings of Christ overflow into our lives, so too does the encouragement we receive through Christ. If we have hardships to undergo, this will contribute to your encouragement and your salvation; if we receive encouragement, this is to gain for you the encouragement which enables you to bear with perseverance the same sufferings as we do. So our hope for you is secure in the knowledge that you share the encouragement we receive, no less than the sufferings we bear. (2 Co 1:3–7)

Imaging

I imagine myself with my group carrying in our hands the decision we made in the Lord.

The grace desired

I ask the Lord to help me discern from my interior movement of spirits whether our decision is confirmed or not confirmed.

Points

I come before the Lord united in my being with our decision.

I recall the image of our communal consolation. Do I sense congruity and continuity with our communal graced history, charism and mission in connection with this decision?

Do I experience this kind of consolation with this decision?

How will I describe the experience that I had as I prayed for confirmation?

Colloquy

I thank the Lord for what happened to me in prayer and I ask God to help me present my experience to the group. The *Lord's Prayer.*

GROUP SHARING

The group recalls an event where it has experienced the consolations of God (unity, beauty, truth, goodness, peace, joy, sorrow, faith, hope, love) and composes itself with Paul's word of 2 Co 1:3–7.

The group shares the experience of private reflection.

The group reflects on what each person has shared quietly for a few minutes.

The group shares what impressed each person as the others shared.

GROUP CONVERSATION WITH THE LORD

The group expresses its belief in God's goodness and presence to it during this process and it prays for guidance to implement the decision correctly. The *Lord's Prayer*.

NOTES

[1] Cf. Patrick O'Sullivan sj: 'A Brief Summary of CLC Spirituality', in *Progressio* (publication of the World Christian Life Community), Rome, January 1987, p. 6. He writes, 'Mission is not so much something we do as the whole quality of presence we bring to the world in which we live.'

[2] Members of groups may be assisted in discovering their personal gifts by answering the Myers-Briggs Type Indicator (MBTI) questionnaire that helps them to know their preferred ways of dealing with the world. See p. 88.

[3] My colleague George Leach sj tells me that among many groups of Native peoples in Canada consensus is achieved through a process of passing a sacred symbol (eagle feather, stone, talking stick) to every person in a sacred circle. Only the person with the sacred symbol may speak. Then the symbol is passed on to the next person who may speak or pass it on. The symbol may be passed around the circle many times until everyone agrees with the decision and action to follow.

[4] See *Facing Your Type*, p. 11 for a full explanation of this process.

[5] Cf. *ISECP* manual, volume 1, pp. 137–45.

THE CONTINUAL WAY OF COMMUNAL SPIRITUAL DISCERNMENT

> . . . the transcendental precepts: be attentive, be intelligent, be reasonable, be responsible and be in love.
>
> (Bernard Lonergan SJ)[1]

Spiritual discernment is not a once-in-a-lifetime experience but a way of life. It is a way of life in active relationship with the mind and heart of the living Christ.

Spiritual discernment involves recognizing the initiative of the Spirit in our experiences and following the Spirit's lead. One prays to grow in awareness of the true significance of experience and to become ever more sensitive in recognizing and following the lead of the Spirit.

It is a continuous activity. Communities living this way of life are constantly going through a process that carries them through choices to decisions and actions. When discernment becomes a way of life for a community it embraces a communal process in the five phases discussed in chapter 3. Members dispose themselves to find the movement of the Spirit in the group's *experience* (phase 1). They privately *reflect* (phase 2) on their experience and then they *articulate* (phase 3) the fruit of their prayer and meditation to the group. Together, members *interpret* (phase 4) the meaning of their experience in terms of their sense of themselves as members of Christ's body. Then the community moves confidently, prayerfully and with careful deliberation into consideration of their future by *deciding on action* (phase 5) that they can freely offer to God because they know it to be in harmony with God's ongoing work of creation. A communal spirituality of discernment reinforces itself and grows as a way of life.

A community which desires to be committed to the betterment

of humanity will constantly heighten its awareness of the movement of spirits within it. It will bring gospel values into its decision-making. It will seek to be open to the Spirit calling it beyond itself for the good of others. It will seek to recognize the forces within and beyond itself which are benevolent to the human enterprise and those forces destructive to the human enterprise. With this in mind the group will reflect on its experiences, articulate its awareness of the movement of spirits, and interpret their directions as true or false calls so that its decisions and actions will be for the upbuilding of humanity rather than its destruction.

After celebrating God's presence with it in an experience of decision-making a community may consider looking afresh at the implications of its desire to love and serve God better in all things. It faces the questions: 'How can we make the discerning of decision and actions our way of life?' 'How can we develop a spirituality of apostolic action?', questions challenging many faith communities today.

Awareness of the ways God has gifted the community during its discernment becomes the foundation for building a discerning community. The appreciation of the ways discernment has fostered community gives the group the desire and resolve to experience communal discernment as its ongoing way of life.

The conviction that this is desirable and possible needs to be more than a theoretical or a 'wouldn't it be nice if' attitude. For communal spiritual discernment to become a way of life the members must have a deep conviction that this is a necessary ideal for them. They realize that this is the way for their community to stay alive and fulfil its deepest desires as a Christian group seeking to be an instrument of God's goodness and love in our world.

Using the processes and exercises suggested in this book ought to give a group a deep conviction that it wants to continue its life in this way, for they are a concrete experience of communal discernment, and such experience raises hope for the future.

Among these probably the most significant from a spiritual point of view is the group's awareness of its communal spiritual consolation and desolation. It may find that time and time again it has to return to its experiences of the felt presence of God and the felt absence of God in order to foster deep awareness and understanding of how God relates to it. This will probably mean that the group

177

will return often to its history line and its covenant or mission statement. Continual reflection on the impact of these processes on the group raises consciousness of the various 'movements of spirits' taking place in all the aspects of its communal life. The group keeps calling itself to a heightened awareness of the movement of spirits in its members at all times. In doing this it more fully appropriates its experiences of communal spiritual consolation and desolation.

The conviction then arises that there is a constant movement of spirits from within and from beyond the group at all times. Now it is ready to practise the formalized exercise of communal spiritual awareness. It realizes that communal discernment can be a way of life for the group. It is ready to seek to recognize God in all things and co-operate with the discerned presence of God supporting, calling, leading and encouraging it in all things.

Heightening awareness

The processes and exercises described in previous chapters are instruments which can help a group fulfil its desire to grow in awareness of spiritual consolation and desolation. Those exercises dealing directly with the community's communal graced history can help it appreciate the constant presence of God to it in an intimate and affectionate way. The process of discerning correct decisions will bring forth an in-depth understanding of spiritual consolation and desolation given to it from within and from beyond the group.

Different methods of prayer – such as brief or lengthy communal awareness exercises – can heighten the awareness of God's presence in the group to assure the living of a communal discerning way of life.

Brief awareness exercises can take place at any time during a gathering of the community. They can happen spontaneously as members become quiet for reflection on what is taking place in and among them.

In a more formal lengthy communal awareness exercise the community will spend time reflecting on its interior state of being and on its apostolic life. It will reflect on the ways God is present to it in its ongoing history. It will reflect on the various gifts of each member and the ways the members interchange with each other. It will consider its location in the life-death-resurrection cycle. It will question its use of the energy cycle. It will wonder about the interior and exterior spirits moving it. It will recognize if it is with the Lord in suffering and joy. It will seek to find God in all things. It will give thanks for God's gifts, and express sorrow for the times it has failed to respond to the call of the Spirit in its experiences.

A way of life for individuals

Individuals develop a discerning way of life by using Ignatius' method of the daily examen. (See note 3, chapter 2, p. 44.) This involves examining one's day from a spiritual point of view. For one's daily examen Ignatius suggests the five activities of *thanksgiving, prayer for light*, the *examen* itself – a review, hour by hour, of the period under consideration – *responses* of sorrow or joy, and *resolution* or *prayer* to be free to respond more fully to God's initiatives in the immediate future (Exx 43). It is easy to recognize that these parallel the five phases of discernment.

Thanksgiving and the prayer for light compose the person for the activity of examining one's day. They are also instruments for composing oneself to enter the phases of *experience* and *reflection*. Ignatius' daily examen combines the *articulation* and *interpretation* of the five phases. The responses and resolution combine the *decision and action* phase.

Daily Examen	Five Phases of Discernment	Communal Awareness
Thanksgiving. Prayer for Light		Community composes itself.
	Experience	Community tells its story.

179

Examen	Reflection	Community reflects on its story.
	Articulation	Community indicates what impressed it.
	Interpretation	Community discerns the spirits moving it.
Responses	Decision and Action	Community responds with sorrow and/or joy.
Resolution		Community considers significance for decision-making.

A way of life for communities

Communities can promote a discerning way of life by using a method similar to Ignatius' daily examen. A communal awareness exercise would involve thanksgiving and prayer for light as a preliminary. For a community this is the composing of the group as it begins this prayer. The group puts itself into a foundational attitude of thanksgiving before God for its existence and continual preservation. Knowing its limitations and tendencies to deception it seeks from God the grace to be enlightened.

After this it recalls both the individual and communal experience since its last meeting. Individuals tell their stories. After their sharing the community reflects on the communal viewpoint. This leads the community into interpreting its experience in terms of the movement of spirits. Now it may respond to the Lord and itself in acts of sorrow and joy. Then it begins to consider how these experiences are calling it forth into the future. This leads it to face further decisions and actions.

This exercise may take place in a brief way at the end of each meeting or in a more extended way a few times each year. Time will be needed in each meeting for a brief evaluation at the end. Communities often use a more extended communal awareness exercise at the end of significant stages in their development, perhaps while making a serious communal decision, at the end of a year, or possibly before a summer break.

A brief awareness exercise

The evaluation at the end of each meeting can be a brief communal awareness exercise. Its purpose is to raise some awareness of our response to or rejection of the presence of God with the community in the previous week and during this meeting. It will be a reflection with two aspects: each person's sense of the meeting and the activity of God during the meeting.

A lengthy awareness exercise

When a community wishes for a more lengthy experience of awareness it will spend one complete meeting doing it. Then it will give the necessary time for reflection and sharing on each of the five activities that Ignatius gives for the daily examen, thanksgiving, prayer for light, the examen itself, acts of sorrow and joy, and resolution.

Thanksgiving and the prayer for light: These are preliminary. They are similar to the introduction of each meeting when the community composes itself through a hymn, scripture reading and prayer. At this meeting the hymn, scripture and prayer express an attitude of gratitude for God's continual care and preservation. The grace that it seeks from God is that of light. The community asks the Holy Spirit to enlighten it to recognize and understand the various movements of spirits it has been experiencing since the last time it spent one complete meeting doing a communal awareness exercise. To accomplish this review may take some time for often we do not recognize what have been the interior experiences and which forces are at work in the community.

The Examen: After these preliminaries the community moves to the Examen. It will spend some time in quiet reflection upon its experience since the last time it made an extensive communal examen. This will entail finding those special gifts of communal consolation as well as its experience of communal desolation. Then it will tell its story.

To do this it might compose or return to its history line, recording on a large piece of newsprint some of the decisive events since it has been together or adding those that have happened since the last time it did such a complete communal awareness. It will now discuss why these events are significant. It will look for patterns of God's love and patterns of members' responses or rejections, and discern the movement of spirits that it recognizes.

Some of the criteria that the community might use to make these judgements are contained in its vision, dreams and desires, and in its various statements of goals and objectives. These will help the community judge whether it is responding or not to its communal call from God.

In discussion members can make definite reference to the group's interior life and some to its apostolic life. Referring to its objectives can help the community judge how it has grown spiritually in appreciation of all the members or how it has neglected its own spiritual growth. The community will be able to recognize where and how it has been an instrument of God's love and care for our wounded world and where and how it has failed to answer God's call to it in this regard.

Acts of sorrow and joy: The community is now in a position to respond to God's activity in its life by acts of sorrow and joy. It will recognize those times it has failed to respond to the love of God within its own interior life and in its apostolate. It can then make suitable acts of sorrow to God and to itself. Similarly it will recognize those occasions when it has responded to God's love calling it beyond itself in its own life and in the apostolate. This will stir up acts of joy and thanksgiving to God and to itself.

Resolution: With this communal awareness of the activity of God in its interior and exterior life the community can now recognize a present call to it. It may realize that a communal issue has surfaced; in this case it can follow the steps (pages 29–35) and proceed to the fifth phase of decision-and-action. Ongoing communal discernment is a communal spirituality of action. Without this phase the previous phases are truncated. A commitment to apostolic action allows the community to become a cell of the church bringing gospel service to the whole of humanity.

EXERCISE XIV: BRIEF EVALUATION AT THE END OF EACH MEETING

The purpose of this exercise is to raise some awareness of how God has been with us during the meeting and our response to or rejection of the presence of God.

Composition

All consider quietly that they are in the presence of God. They take on an attitude of thanksgiving and seek the light of the Holy Spirit to discern the significance of this meeting. The following questions might help: 1. How did I feel about the meeting? 2. How do I sense God being with us during this meeting? 3. How are we to respond?

Communal sharing

Only a brief answer is necessary to the first question. The second and third questions may require more extended sharing and discussion.

Prayer

A communal prayer of thanksgiving for God's continual presence with the community is in order. End with the *Lord's Prayer*.

EXERCISE XV: A FULL MEETING OF COMMUNAL AWARENESS[2]

The exercise begins with a quiet act of presence of God in and with the community. 'Let us begin by placing ourselves in the presence of the Trinity. We try to become aware of God *beholding* us . . . .'

Thanksgiving

Aware of our poverty before the Lord we reflect upon all of God's gifts to us – those that we are grateful for and those we find it difficult to be grateful for.

Let us express our thanks to the Lord as a community. (Mention those gifts for which we wish to give thanks today.)

Prayer for guidance of the Spirit

We ask for the guidance of the Spirit to give us a growing insight into the mystery that we are. ('Spirit of the living God, fall afresh on us . . .' could be sung.)

Examination

With the Spirit leading, we try to get in touch with what has been happening in us and through us during this meeting so that we will be able to share these awarenesses in the community.

- Sense of presence: to God within and beyond us
                        to each other.

- Communication: How did we express and listen to each other? Did we complete the communications loop?

- Use of time: Did we start and end on time? Did we use the agenda responsibly and freely?

- Use of instruments of communal discernment: Life Cycle, Energy Cycle, Pastoral Cycle, Hidden Forces, (Inclusivity vs. Exclusivity), Decision-Making Process.

- Questions:

  Did we acknowledge each other's personality profiles? Did we call upon the different gifts in the group? Did we follow the SNTF functions of the MBTI as we moved to decision?

  Did we follow the energy cycle of Action – Evaluation – Recommendation – Decision – Action as we discerned?

  After the decision a group might check if it has followed the energy cycle to everyone's satisfaction.

  Did we locate ourselves on the life cycle?

  Did we recall our unique experiences and patterns of communal spiritual consolation?

Thanks, contrition and sorrow

Recognition of the Lord's working within us. Awareness of and sorrow for placing obstacles to the Spirit's working in our communal life.

Mention those things for which you wish to express thanks. 'Glory be to God . . .'.

Mention those for which you wish to ask forgiveness from God and the community . . . 'Lord, have mercy'.

Hopeful attitude toward the future

Let us become aware of better communal discernment process for our future gatherings and ask the Lord's grace to help us co-operate.

Close with the *Lord's Prayer*.

NOTES

[1]*Method in Theology* (Herder and Herder, New York, 1977), p. 55.
[2]This is based on an exercise developed by Sr Frances MacDougall CND, in *A Manual of Formation for Christian Life Community*, Phase I (Guelph, Ontario, 1992), p. R114.

11

CELEBRATING A CONTINUOUS LIFE OF
COMMUNAL INTIMACY WITH GOD

'Blessed are those who are invited to the marriage supper of the lamb.'
(Rv 19:9)

When a community has had the experience of God's presence to it through its beginnings, growth, development and decision-making stages it feels the need to take these experiences into itself in gratitude, expectation and anticipation. It wishes to celebrate its intimate relationship with God and commit itself to continue living in spiritual intimacy with God.

St Ignatius suggests two ways to celebrate God's giftedness to us in our interior life: the 'application of the senses' to the mysteries of Christ's life presented to us in the gospels and 'A Contemplation to Attain the Love of God' over the mystery of our own life. As the Eucharist is the paradigm of celebration for Christians so it can be used here as an example of the application of the senses.

The Eucharist as paradigm

CELEBRATION

We might see the Eucharist in terms of four movements: *remembering* God's marvellous acts, *sensing* God's continual presence, *appreciating* the great labour of Christ's passion, death and resurrection for us, and *going forth* with hope and energy to be instruments of God's love in our world. We recall God's great actions as the word of God in the scriptures is broken open. We sense God's presence to us as we present ourselves with the gifts of bread and wine. We enter into the labour of God with the words of Christ at the Last Supper. We are filled with hope and energy as we experience our unity with each other at communion.

It is important that these four movements be present in an atmosphere of celebration. The 1989 film *Babette's Feast* is an inspiring example of how the Eucharist can be celebrated. In it we see two sisters who showed kindness to Babette when she was destitute in a foreign land. Later Babette gains a large sum of money. She spends it all to gather food and wine for a feast for the two sisters and their friends. She takes a long time preparing the meal. It becomes her work of art. We see her enjoying the pleasure of watching the guests eat and drink her creations. The guests experience reconciliation and union with each other as they share the feast. There is gratitude and joy, singing and dancing.

We do many of these things when we celebrate. We gather, we spend time with each other, we tell stories about ourselves, we prepare our feast, we eat and drink, we sing and dance. We go home renewed, energized and at peace with each other and God.

AN EXPERIENCE

I have been at celebrations of the Eucharist in which similar experiences took place. In one particular celebration, the group gathered, at first somewhat uneasy and shy with each other since they last met. The children and adults then began the ritual of preparing the meal. Much time was given to making chapattis and cleaning lentils for soup. At the more formal gathering for the Eucharist everyone shared their stories of God's presence with them since the last meeting. It was truly a sharing of the word of God. They recounted their surprise at the working of God in their lives since the last meeting. These stories were followed by the scriptural story of Christ. We sang songs of praise and thanksgiving. The Eucharist itself took place at the table where the feast was to follow. There was a ritualized dance of adoration. The kiss of peace often included many persons in one embrace. Communion followed. After the closing prayers of the Eucharist the group began eating and drinking the feast they had prepared earlier. Dancing and song continued the celebration until the group dispersed to their homes. There were

187

departing gestures of joy and anticipation of coming together again to celebrate their union with each other in Christ.

The interior senses in communal celebration

In classical spirituality authors speak about the spiritual or interior senses. They are referring to experiences that we can have of God that can best be described in terms of our senses. They write, for example, about smelling the infinite fragrance of God, tasting the divine sweetness, and touching the virtues of Christ, Mary and the saints (cf. Exx 122–5).

The experience is related to spiritual consolation in which there is an increase of faith, hope and love. As faith increases we are given the power to hear and see as not before. As hope increases our being is filled with fragrance. As love increases we can touch and taste our union with God.

The scriptural writers of the Hebrew Testament could write in this way from their individual experiences of the Spirit: 'Taste and see that Yahweh is good' (Ps 34:8); 'How pleasant your promise to my palate, sweeter than honey in my mouth' (Ps 119:103).

We are given an awareness of the presence of God that is many-coloured, full of song, sweet, fragrant and touching. It is similar to the sense of presence that I have of another person that is beyond what I see, hear, smell, taste or touch. The experience of a person is more than what the exterior senses give. It is also more than intellectual abstraction from the sense data. It is a loving experience.

The body of Christ

In contemplating, Ignatius suggests that we use the active imagination on a gospel event of the life of Jesus Christ. Through imaginatively seeing and hearing the persons and actions of the gospel story we can become present at the event. In the midst of this imagining Ignatius suggests that we 'reflect on myself (ourselves), that I (we) may derive some profit' (Exx 114). We may dwell in the presence by use of the imagination which draws us into our intimate relation-

188

ship with God to the extent that we can touch, hear, smell, 'taste and see' the goodness of the Lord and the other divine attributes.

By this faith-filled method, we enter into the gospel story using our active imagination. Then the risen Christ through the activity of the Holy Spirit in us may make his presence known to us in a special way. This presence may draw us into a deeper awareness or affective understanding of ourselves, others and Jesus Christ. We may be given an intimate 'knowing of the love of Christ which is beyond all knowledge' (Ep 3:19) and become instruments of God's grace in our world.

The basis for such a communal awareness is the Holy Spirit communicating through the humanity of Jesus the ineffable presence of God. Jesus himself was the Word that his disciples and friends were able to see, hear and touch.

> Something which has existed from the beginning,
> which we have heard,
> which we have seen with our own eyes,
> which we have watched
> and touched with our own hands,
> the Word of life –
> this is our theme.
> That life was made visible;
> we saw it and are giving our testimony,
> declaring to you the eternal life,
> which was present to the Father
> and has been revealed to us.
> We are declaring to you
> what we have seen and heard,
> that you too may share our life.
> Our life is shared with the Father
> and with his Son Jesus Christ.
> We are writing this to you so that our joy may be complete.
>   (1 Jn 1:1–4)

In the Christian understanding of such experiences the mystery of the incarnation is central. 'The Word became flesh' (Jn 1:14) juxtaposes the divine and the human. So the applying of the interior senses is a way of praying that seeks an awareness in one's inner being of the divine in us. The sentiment that inspires the Nepali greeting *Nameste*, which means 'I greet the divine in you', is appreciated in a special way. Through this instrument we can gain a heightened awareness of Christ in our midst.

One of the effects of the historical expression of God in the incarnation of Jesus is the experience of God's particular presence to us, creating, sustaining, calling us forth in freedom to salvation and co-responsibility for the betterment of humanity. In the days Jesus walked the earth this was experienced in the particular personal presence of Jesus touching and speaking to people: 'Your faith has saved you' (Lk 7:50; 8:48,50; 17:19; 18:42). During the years of his own ministry Jesus extended his presence to others by sending the apostles and disciples to preach the good news and cure people.

Risen Christ

The humanity of Jesus does not disappear with his resurrection. The authors of the Christian Testament, especially St Paul, insist that the faithful are an expression of the body of Christ: 'Do you not realize that your bodies are members of Christ's body' (1 Co 6:15); 'Now Christ's body is yourselves, each of you with a part to play in the whole' (1 Co 12:27). But to know this requires the vision of faith. We need eyes to see and ears to hear. The application of the interior senses can help us at this point. We can use it to recognize and appreciate the presence of Christ in our communal experiences.

After his resurrection this presence was known in various experiences of the early church. It was known in the fellowship experience of believers in their communal expressions of prayer and sharing. The material experience of the sacraments of baptism and Eucharist intensified this experience of the Christ-community. The action of the Holy Spirit gave the faithful a sense of the real presence of the risen Christ in its members. Paul expressed this by using the phrase 'the body of Christ' many times in his letters.[1] So we today are given a similar real expression of God's presence to us when we gather together in faith. The Eucharist is creative and sustaining

190

and calls us forth in freedom to salvation and co-responsibility for the betterment of humanity.

EXERCISE XVI: APPLYING OUR SENSES TO THE EUCHARISTIC CELEBRATION

A most obvious communal experience of the senses occurs at the eucharistic celebration of the community. We become conscious of the Body of Christ in the gathered faith community. We can even see, hear, touch, smell and taste in this celebration the wondrous work of God for us. In faith we see Christ in each other. We hear the word of God in the scripture. We smell the fragrance of prayer. We touch and taste Christ at the kiss of peace and at communion. These exterior sense experiences can be the commencement of an experience of the interior senses. When this use of the senses brings an experience of the presence of Christ's wisdom, compassion, beauty, gentleness, enfolding, nurturing, strength, dedication, love, sacrifice or joy among the assembly the interior senses are operative.

PREPARATION FOR THIS EXERCISE

Context

> And all of us, with unveiled faces, seeing the glory of the Lord as though reflected in a mirror, are being transformed into the same image from one degree of glory to another. (2 Co 3:18 GNB)

Imaging

We image ourselves with Christ and all Christians gathered around the table of the Lord. Christ is building the realm of God.

Will and desire

An intimate knowledge of Christ made present to us in the celebration of the Eucharist.

191

POINTS: WHILE PRESENT AT THE EUCHARIST

Moving from the physical senses to the spiritual senses:

Eyes: Watch the flickering candle. Observe the various people participating in the celebration. See the light of their desire. Contemplate the light of Christ that they are.

Ears: Hear what is being sung and said. Listen to harmony that is present in the community. Contemplate the song that is their agreement in Christ.

Tongue: Taste the bread and wine. Taste the goodness that is the worshipping community. Contemplate the feast that is the assembly of the community.

Nostrils: Smell the incense and candles. Smell the bouquet of the giftedness of the community. Contemplate the sweetness of gifting each other in Christ.

Hands: Touch each other at the kiss of peace. Touch the texture of the various personalities in the community. Touch Christ's humility in coming to us in each other.

AFTER THE CELEBRATION

Rest with what has been given. Share with each other the intimate sense of Christ's presence to you in the celebration of the Eucharist.

Colloquy

Gather together an expression of appreciation for the sense of Christ in the faith community. The *Lord's Prayer*.

Sing Marty Haugen's: 'Gather us in' (*Gather*, GIA Publications, Chicago, IL, 1988).

Other spiritual celebrations of community

As in the Eucharist other celebrations of community can be presented in four movements: remembering God's marvellous acts in
our lives, sensing God's continual presence to us, appreciating the
ways God works in and with us, and going forth with hope and
energy to be instruments of God's love in our world. We tell the
stories of our experience of God in our lives. We sense God's presence to us through the giftedness of the other members of our
community. We commit ourselves to work with Christ in bringing
the word of encouragement to the world. Our hearts are full of hope
and desire as we experience our unity with each other.

Contemplating its own mystery

A group may wish to contemplate its own mystery in the same way
that Ignatius describes in the Contemplation to Attain the Love of
God (Exx 230–7). In this contemplation Ignatius suggests that we
pray with our own life as we would pray on a mystery of Christ's
life. When a community does this it will enter into its own story
through its faith-filled memory and realize how God loves it and
calls it forth. Continuing in this presence it may now use its external
senses, first to recognize the special gifts of God to it in its membership and second to realize the social implications of these gifts. It
may come to a communal knowledge of itself as a unified body
before God. And if it dwells in this state it may be drawn to a
deeper knowledge of Christ in the community and again be able to
touch, hear, smell, 'taste and see the goodness of the Lord' in the
community.

Celebration in a Christian community flows from a deep appreciation of the many ways God has been, is, and will continue to be
intimate with us. Appreciation begins with remembering and moves
to a sense of presence. It recognizes the great labours and love of
Christ for us and realizes that God will always be with us in the
future.

When a group is not able to participate in the Eucharist there
are other ways and rituals for celebrating God's giftedness to them.

All of these bring about a sense of peace and joy. The fellowship enjoyed flows from a oneness of desire, experience and achievement. These usually involve some form of story-telling.

Story-telling

A group might begin by telling stories of how the different members have gifted the community. Then it might proceed to tell stories about its own beginnings, growth and development. It might recall its efforts to discern a particular action. In these ways it realizes the ways God called it into being and sustained it. It realizes its sinfulness and sense of being called beyond itself to become a grace-filled community and an instrument of God's love in the world. This can fill it with gratitude and the desire to love and serve God in all things.

Further reflection may bring the group to recount the ways God has energized it. This might strengthen its belief that the Holy Spirit is present to it and constantly calling it forth as an instrument of grace for others.

Sense of presence

We usually begin with our sense knowledge, then move to our intellectual knowledge, then to the interpersonal dimension, and eventually we realize that God includes all these and is beyond them. So we speak of God as the Totally Other, as Always Greater, as All Knowing and All Present. Christian revelation indicates that the unity of God is contained in the mystery of a community of three persons. One way people have tried to express our relationship with God is in terms of the One, Beautiful, True and Good.

We might start with an awareness with our exterior senses as we search for a sense of our oneness in Christ and of the One who is God. The communal experience might begin with physical sense of everyone in the room together (holding hands while praying, looking and listening to one person, or eyes closed in prayer) and move through an awareness that these persons are seeking a union of

194

minds and hearts, no matter how diverse their gifts and opinions, to a sense of the one Spirit filling all together. What goes with this sense of oneness? With this oneness a group has a 'common purpose and a common mind' which shows up in a seeking together and a listening attitude to each other. These move further into an experience of all-togetherness. The group may now sense the divine unity of itself with Christ as head of the body.

Coming to the communal experience of the Beautiful might begin with the physical sensation of beauty and move to the beauty of the persons, however unbecoming in physical appearance and manners, and eventually to the sense of God's beauty imbuing the whole communal experience. This sense of the beautiful recognizes a certain simplicity, candour, openness and wonder in the members. From this the community comes to a sense of the divine beauty in the group – 'to enlighten them with the knowledge of God's glory, the glory on the face of Christ' (2 Co 4:6).

How will the communal experience of the True be experienced? It might begin with a nodding of heads and raising of hands in consent and move to an experience of the significance of the persons in themselves and their significance to the group. It might then move to an affective knowledge that 'we are the beloved of God'. Such a sense of the true brings a certain humility, amazement, surprise, commitment and freedom for action. The group senses in itself the words of Christ: 'I am the Way, the Truth and the Life' (Jn 14:6).

A sense of general goodness in the surroundings (comfort, colour, food and drink) might begin a sense of the Good. This might move to the goodness of the persons present, recognizing their deep desire to give generously and reach out in love and appreciation of everyone. There is a certain openness to recognize the goodness of all, seeing everyone as a child of God. The group recognizes that its goodness is part of the goodness of God who has given Christ to the world. 'Indeed, from his fullness we have, all of us, received – yes, one gift replacing another . . . No one has ever seen God; it is the only Son, who is close to the Father's heart, who has made God known' (Jn 1:16–18).

Working with God

It is helpful for a community to recall its experiences of suffering with Christ. It can focus on those experiences where it realized that only the strength of Christ sustained it when it was dealing with suffering within its own group or when it suffered from outside forces. The group may also realize that the labour of perseverance at meetings and commitment to a difficult apostolic action were the result of God's grace. When Jesus was facing the great labour of his life, his passion and death, he was able to proclaim: 'I have glorified you on earth by finishing the work that you gave me to do' (Jn 17:4). The group can appreciate Jesus' words: 'In all truth, I tell you, whoever believes in me will perform the same works as I do myself, and will perform even greater works, because I am going to the Father' (Jn 14:12).

Gifted from God

At times the community recognizes experiences of transformation. It knows that it has achieved attitudes and actions beyond itself. A new awareness of the graced life has been given. The Magnificat of Mary, echoing the Hebrew Testament, expresses the awareness of the group. They know from their experience the truth of the Beatitudes in chapter 5 of Matthew. The experiences of the gifts of the Spirit can fill them with joy and hope in the power of God on their behalf.

EXERCISE XVII: A CONTEMPLATION OF COMMUNAL LOVE[2]

Being taken up into the love of God with our whole community

This exercise is to help the community contemplate the mystery of its own intimate relationship with God. Its desire is to be filled with gratitude and surprise at God's unique relationship with it. It does this by getting in touch with the concrete, historical ways God has been with it, constantly calling it forth into new life.

The exercise has three elements: private prayer, sharing the results of private prayer, and a final appreciation of what has been given to it in prayer and sharing.

PRIVATE PRAYER

Contextualizing

The love and learning we have given to others and to our group and the love and learning we have shared from the Trinity.

Imaging

We image ourselves with all those who have brought us together into our group and encouraged us to work with Christ in building the realm of God.

Will and desire

We want and desire an intimate knowledge and joy of God present in all things, so that we may grow in gratitude for all God's gifts and appreciate the presence of Christ with us calling us forth in freedom and strength to build God's realm on earth.

Pointing

I remember the many blessings that we as a group have shared and recalled in our graced history (light, shadow, call and hope).

I consider the constant presence of God in the larger human experience of geography and history as we attempted to read the signs of the times with Jesus.

I think of our communal responsibility for our world and recall the various sufferings and works we have experienced as co-labourers and co-sufferers with Christ in the human enterprise.

I look at the times we have appreciated and celebrated the grace of God coming to us in simple human goodness and dedication and the transformation of evil by good.

Colloquy

I thank the Lord for what happened to me in prayer and I ask God to help me present my experience to the group. The *Lord's Prayer*.

SHARING

The group shares the fruits of prayer.

APPRECIATION

Further quiet reflection with the following:

- I look anew at each member of our group and sense the presence of the Holy Spirit in each one and in our group as a whole.
- I consider the many labours that we have shared together in Christ and the ways in which Christ has called us into his own passion and suffering for the kingdom.
- Once again I open my mind and heart to appreciate how God has given us a sense of our identity, vocation and mission.

Further brief sharing leading to conversation with the Lord.

The group gathers its sentiment in the form of a prayer of offering and commitment to the Lord.

Group colloquy

An expression of intimate joy and union in the Lord.

NOTES

[1] Cf. Rm 7:14, 12:5, 1 Co 6:15, 10:16, 12:27, 15:19, 20, 22, 23, 31, 2 Co 5:10, 12:2, Ep 3:6, 4:12, 5:23, Ph 1:20, Col 1:24, 2:5, 11, 3:15, 1 Th 5:23, Heb 10:5,10
[2] Cf. *ISECP* manual, volume 1, pp. 189–90.

GENERAL INDEX

action, spirituality of responsible 111, 131ff
Adam-Jesus analogy 3, 100
angels, good and bad 29, 150f
'application of the senses' 5, 188ff, 191f
articulation in process of discernment 29, 32f, 176
Augustine, St 16, 24, 58
authority 134
awareness exercises (examen) 36, 44f, 178f, 180ff, 183ff

Beatitudes 139f, 196
body of Christ 2, 17, 63, 156, 188f
bonding 80

celebration 5, 186ff
Church, early 10, 12, 14, 81
communal dimension: of Ignatian spirituality ix; of faith 1, 11; of personhood 3
community, Christian x, xi, 3, 7ff; survey of 8f; motives for 10ff; in relation to Church 12ff; images of 13f; spirituality of 14, 79ff; identity of 15ff; and covenant 18ff; establishing 59ff; life-style of 81ff; expression of 83f; discernment process of 131ff
companionship, spirituality of 142
confirmation 4f, 83, 149, 155ff
consensus 2, 164ff

consolation 3, 4, 17, 24, 26, 28, 29, 33f, 36, 46ff, 48ff; communal spiritual consolation 51ff, 56ff, 63, 67f, 73, 84, 98ff, 111, 112, 117, 135f, 150, 155f, 159, 162f, 177, 188
contemplation 110ff, 116ff, 124; Ignatian 119; communal 125ff, 128ff, 197ff
Contemplation to Attain the Love of God 193
contemplative experience of sharing story 65
conversion xi, 15, 31, 62, 79, 144
co-operation 92
corporate person 2f, 74
covenant relationship 1, 18f
creatureliness 91f, 95, 98

decision and action x, 4, 5, 16, 29, 35, 84, 117, 142, 176
decision-making 91, 116, 142ff, 148
desolation 3, 17, 24, 28, 33f, 36, 50, 85, 95ff, 103, 135, 157, 177
director, spiritual 94
discernment, spiritual 25ff; communal 3, 4, 39f, 46ff, 50f, 75, 136f; as a way of life 5, 36, 176ff; purposes of 29f, 37f; dynamic of 29; process of 29ff, 38, 131ff, 155ff; example of 36; individual

201

REFERENCES TO THE SPIRITUAL EXERCISES

BIBLICAL REFERENCES